Glass, Irony and God

for my
mother
and father

Glass, Irony & God

Anne Carson

introduction by

Guy Davenport

A NEW DIRECTIONS BOOK

Acknowledgments: Grateful acknowledgment is made to the editors and publishers of magazines in which some of the poems in this book first appeared: *American Poetry Review, New Feminist Research, Raritan,* and *Thamyris.*
A modified version of "The Fall of Rome" appeared in *The Descant Anthology* (McClelland & Stewart, Toronto, 1995).

Manufactured in the United States of America.

First published as New Directions Paperbook 808 in 1995.

Library of Congress Cataloging-in-Publication Data

Carson, Anne, 1950–
Glass, irony, and God / Anne Carson : introduction by Guy Davenport.
p. cm.
ISBN 0-8112-1302-1 (alk. paper)
I. Title.
PS3553.A7667G53 1995
813′.54—dc20 95-30637
CIP

ISBN-13: 978-0-8112-1302-8

New Directions Books are published for James Laughlin
by New Directions Publishing Corporation
80 Eighth Avenue, New York 10011

20 19 18 17

TABLE OF CONTENTS

INTRODUCTION

Anne Carson begins her *Eros the Bittersweet* (1986), a book about love and learning, with a fragment of Kafka's in which *ein Philosoph* tries to catch spinning tops, "for he believed that the understanding of any detail, that of a spinning top for instance, was sufficient for the understanding of all things." *War die kleinste Kleinigkeit wirklich erkannt, dann war alles erkannt.* Our planet spins on its axis; atoms spin; the liveliest equilibrium seems to require vertigo. An earlier *Philosoph* who also liked to be around playing boys thought that Eros, himself a boy, was necessary to philosophy, a *love* of learning. Behind Kafka's *Der Kreisel,* half a page long, are Greek boys tossing knucklebones, watched by Sokrates, who knows that as long as they are playing their minds are spinning and alive and open to intelligent questioning.

What we learn from *Eros the Bittersweet* while being spun alive by its brilliance is that its author is a philosopher of much cunning and an agile reader, a scholar with a mind as fresh as a spring meadow, no dust anywhere on her. Classicists tend to be a sprightly lot. Erasmus was as charming a person as God makes them. A. E. Housman, now that we know his secret life, vied with Norman Douglas for being the last authentic pagan. My first Greek teacher, James Nardin Truesdale, had swum, mother-naked, many laps of the pool in the Duke gym, before he met our eight o'clock class. At our very first meeting he strode in and said in the voice of a drill sergeant that the first letter of the Greek alphabet is *alpha,* the second *beta,* the third *gamma.*

My second text by Anne Carson was an article in a learned journal, "Echo with No Door on Her Mouth: A Notional Refraction through Sophokles, Plato, and Defoe." Defoe! There are classicists whose writing is just short of terrifying to read (Zuntz, Kirk, Cunningham, and Page for starters). Bringers of the Law down from Olympos are stern and earnest men, and they carry a cane to deal with Eros should he show his impudent face. Yet it is precisely the classicists who see our culture as one among many (Greece, like ancient Israel, was a traffic circle of belligerently different peoples, and Rome was a United States of meddlers in all the affairs of the world) and who are least embarrassed by the pagan topsoil in which our culture still grows its garden.

The past for the classicist is simply another room in the house, as familiar as any other. Jane Harrison grew up with a county father who intrepidly, for grace before meals, said, "For what we are about to receive, may the Lord be truly thankful." Both Zeus and Yahweh would have seen nothing askew in this prayer, and little Jane grew up to be a diligent explicator of Greek ritual. In Anne Carson's poetry we are everywhere looking into depths, through transparences of time and place. As with Virginia Woolf, she gives us scenes—moors, rooms, orchards, deserts—in which vivid action holds our attention.

Poets distinguish themselves by the way they see. A dull poet is one who sees fashionably or blindly what he thinks poets see. The original poet sees with new eyes, or with imported vision (as with Eliot seeing like Laforgue or Pound like the Chinese). Anne Carson's eyes are original. We are not yet used to them and she may seem unpoetic, or joltingly new, like Whitman or Emily Dickinson in their day. She writes in a kind of mathematics of the emotions, with daring equations and recurring sets and subsets of images. As with Matthew Arnold, truth and observation are more important than lyric effect or coloring. If a good line happens, it happens. Anne Carson's poems are like notes made in their pristine urgency, as fresh and bright as a series of sudden remarks. But they are the remarks of a speaker who remains silent until there's something to be said, something that has been processed in the heart and brooded over in the imagination and is not to be further processed in rhyme or meter.

The poem called "Book of Isaiah" may give us a clue as to the circuits of Anne Carson's genius. This is a poem that reminds us of Shulamith Hareven's *Navi* (*Prophet*) in its ability to imagine archaic theology and the deeply primitive *feel* of ancient Judaism. Both Hareven and Carson can enter Old Testament ways of thought and narrative, Hareven into the *numen,* Carson into the human (and even witty) narrative eccentricities of biblical style, a gathering into what sounds like history of disparate events, an oral tradition written down by different chroniclers without regard for sequence or consistency. Carson's Isaiah and Carson's God are both authentically biblical, no libel anywhere. They look wonderfully strange because we were rarely taught to read the bible with an honest mind.

I had begun discovering Anne Carson's poems about the same time as James Laughlin, who knows a poet when he sees one. He alerted me to "a poem about God that you have to read." Sitting at his back window at Meadow House in Connecticut, from which he observes his flock of sheep and where he writes his own poems and keeps in touch with hundreds of writers whom he has come to know in sixty years of publishing ("the Godfather of Modernism," Andréi Codrescu calls him), Laughlin's knowing eye saw Anne Carson for what she is: a real poet whose poems are unfailingly memorable. Hence this book, which I gather wasn't easy to come by. And then this inadequate introduction, as Laughlin thought "she needs explaining." I don't think she needs explaining at all, but Laughlin has lived through the slow acceptance of his New Directions poets—three decades for William Carlos Williams to advance from small-town doctor who wrote poems between patients, and whom Laughlin was discerning and brave enough to publish, to Old Master—and wants to speed things up. There are probably beguiling ways of going about this far better than anything I might do (I know nothing of Anne Carson except her writing and the stray fact that she is also a fancier of volcanoes and paints them erupting).

The test of poetry, however, is easy. Read "The Glass Essay," a poem richer than most novels nowadays. See how in its utter clarity of narration it weaves and conflates one theme with another, how it works in the Brontës as daimons to preside over the poem and to haunt it, how it tells two strong stories with Tolstoyan skill, how it reflects on its themes in subtle and surprising ways. This is a boldly new kind of poem, but neither its boldness nor its novelty make it good. It is good because of its truth and the sensibility of its telling. These qualities maintain from poem to poem, though no two poems are alike. Anne Carson's powers of invention are apparently infinite. The range of her interests is from horizon to horizon.

It has been the spirit of the arts for most of the century to dare new forms. Joyce's daring is evident on every page he wrote; so are Pound's and Cummings's. Sometimes the daring was more for its own sake (as with about half of Gertrude Stein and much of Picasso) than toward a technique useful to others. Anne Carson's daring succeeds. She is among those who are returning poetry to good strong narrative (as we might expect of a classicist). She shifts attention from repeating stanzaic form (which came about when all poems were songs) to well-contoured blocks of phrases: analogues of paragraphs in prose. Prose will not accommodate Carson's syncopations, her terseness, her deft changes of scene.

She writes philosophy and critical essays that are as beautiful and charming as good poetry; it is not surprising that her poems are philosophical—in the old sense, when from Herakleitos (if his fragments are from a poem) to Lucretius, and even longer (Bernardus, Dante, Cavalcanti), poetry was a way to write philosophy. When Sokrates took Sappho's desire for the young and fused it with the process of learning, sublimating it and disciplining it with stoic restraint, he gave the genius of the West a philosophical idea that lasted almost two thousand years. Desire is now a medical and sociological problem. The god Eros and his mother Aphrodita are outlaws again, a new puritanism descends, but there are still poets—Anne Carson is among them—who allow Eros his dominion and can tell us that while prophets sleep, the asters in the garden unload their red thunder into the dark.

—Guy Davenport

Glass, Irony and God

THE GLASS ESSAY

I

I can hear little clicks inside my dream.
Night drips its silver tap
down the back.
At 4 A.M. I wake. Thinking

of the man who
left in September.
His name was Law.

My face in the bathroom mirror
has white streaks down it.
I rinse the face and return to bed.
Tomorrow I am going to visit my mother.

SHE

She lives on a moor in the north.
She lives alone.
Spring opens like a blade there.
I travel all day on trains and bring a lot of books—

some for my mother, some for me
including *The Collected Works Of Emily Brontë*.
This is my favourite author.

Also my main fear, which I mean to confront.
Whenever I visit my mother
I feel I am turning into Emily Brontë,

my lonely life around me like a moor,
my ungainly body stumping over the mud flats with a look of
transformation
that dies when I come in the kitchen door.
What meat is it, Emily, we need?

THREE

Three silent women at the kitchen table.
My mother's kitchen is dark and small but out the window
there is the moor, paralyzed with ice.
It extends as far as the eye can see

over flat miles to a solid unlit white sky.
Mother and I are chewing lettuce carefully.
The kitchen wall clock emits a ragged low buzz that jumps

once a minute over the twelve.
I have Emily p. 216 propped open on the sugarbowl
but am covertly watching my mother.

A thousand questions hit my eyes from the inside.
My mother is studying her lettuce.
I turn to p. 217.

"In my flight through the kitchen I knocked over Hareton
who was hanging a litter of puppies
from a chairback in the doorway. . . ."

It is as if we have all been lowered into an atmosphere of glass.
Now and then a remark trails through the glass.
Taxes on the back lot. Not a good melon,

too early for melons.
Hairdresser in town found God, closes shop every Tuesday.
Mice in the teatowel drawer again.
Little pellets. Chew off

the corners of the napkins, if they knew
what paper napkins cost nowadays.
Rain tonight.

Rain tomorrow.
That volcano in the Philippines at it again. What's her name
Anderson died no not Shirley

the opera singer. Negress.
Cancer.
Not eating your garnish, you don't like pimento?

Out the window I can see dead leaves ticking over the flatland
and dregs of snow scarred by pine filth.
At the middle of the moor

where the ground goes down into a depression,
the ice has begun to unclench.
Black open water comes

curdling up like anger. My mother speaks suddenly.
That psychotherapy's not doing you much good is it?
You aren't getting over him.

My mother has a way of summing things up.
She never liked Law much
but she liked the idea of me having a man and getting on with life.

Well he's a taker and you're a giver I hope it works out,
was all she said after she met him.
Give and take were just words to me

at the time. I had not been in love before.
It was like a wheel rolling downhill.
But early this morning while mother slept

and I was downstairs reading the part in *Wuthering Heights*
where Heathcliff clings at the lattice in the storm sobbing
Come in! Come in! to the ghost of his heart's darling,

I fell on my knees on the rug and sobbed too.
She knows how to hang puppies,
that Emily.

It isn't like taking an aspirin you know, I answer feebly.
Dr. Haw says grief is a long process.
She frowns. What does it accomplish

all that raking up the past?
Oh—I spread my hands—
I prevail! I look her in the eye.
She grins. Yes you do.

WHACHER

Whacher,
Emily's habitual spelling of this word,
has caused confusion.
For example

in the first line of the poem printed *Tell me, whether, is it winter?*
in the Shakespeare Head edition.
But whacher is what she wrote.

Whacher is what she was.
She whached God and humans and moor wind and open night.
She whached eyes, stars, inside, outside, actual weather.

She whached the bars of time, which broke.
She whached the poor core of the world,
wide open.

To be a whacher is not a choice.
There is nowhere to get away from it,
no ledge to climb up to—like a swimmer

who walks out of the water at sunset
shaking the drops off, it just flies open.
To be a whacher is not in itself sad or happy,

although she uses these words in her verse
as she uses the emotions of sexual union in her novel,
grazing with euphemism the work of whaching.

But it has no name.
It is transparent.
Sometimes she calls it Thou.

"Emily is in the parlour brushing the carpet,"
records Charlotte in 1828.
Unsociable even at home

and unable to meet the eyes of strangers when she ventured out,
Emily made her awkward way
across days and years whose bareness appalls her biographers.

This sad stunted life, says one.
Uninteresting, unremarkable, wracked by disappointment
and despair, says another.

She could have been a great navigator if she'd been male,
suggests a third. Meanwhile
Emily continued to brush into the carpet the question,

Why cast the world away.
For someone hooked up to Thou,
the world may have seemed a kind of half-finished sentence.

But in between the neighbour who recalls her
coming in from a walk on the moors
with her face "lit up by a divine light"

and the sister who tells us
Emily never made a friend in her life,
is a space where the little raw soul

slips through.
It goes skimming the deep keel like a storm petrel,
out of sight.

The little raw soul was caught by no one.
She didn't have friends, children, sex, religion, marriage, success, a salary
or a fear of death. She worked

in total six months of her life (at a school in Halifax)
and died on the sofa at home at 2 P.M. on a winter afternoon
in her thirty-first year. She spent

most of the hours of her life brushing the carpet,
walking the moor
or whaching. She says

it gave her peace.
"All tight and right in which condition it is to be hoped we shall all be this day 4 years,"
she wrote in her Diary Paper of 1837.

Yet her poetry from beginning to end is concerned with prisons,
vaults, cages, bars, curbs, bits, bolts, fetters,
locked windows, narrow frames, aching walls.

"Why all the fuss?" asks one critic.
"She wanted liberty. Well didn't she have it?
A reasonably satisfactory homelife,

a most satisfactory dreamlife—why all this beating of wings?
What was this cage, invisible to us,
which she felt herself to be confined in?"

Well there are many ways of being held prisoner,
I am thinking as I stride over the moor.
As a rule after lunch mother has a nap

and I go out to walk.
The bare blue trees and bleached wooden sky of April
carve into me with knives of light.

Something inside it reminds me of childhood—
it is the light of the stalled time after lunch
when clocks tick

and hearts shut
and fathers leave to go back to work
and mothers stand at the kitchen sink pondering

something they never tell.
You remember too much,
my mother said to me recently.

Why hold onto all that? And I said,
Where can I put it down?
She shifted to a question about airports.

Crops of ice are changing to mud all around me
as I push on across the moor
warmed by drifts from the pale blue sun.

On the edge of the moor our pines
dip and coast in breezes
from somewhere else.

Perhaps the hardest thing about losing a lover is
to watch the year repeat its days.
It is as if I could dip my hand down

into time and scoop up
blue and green lozenges of April heat
a year ago in another country.

I can feel that other day running underneath this one
like an old videotape—here we go fast around the last corner
up the hill to his house, shadows

of limes and roses blowing in the car window
and music spraying from the radio and him
singing and touching my left hand to his lips.

Law lived in a high blue room from which he could see the sea.
Time in its transparent loops as it passes beneath me now
still carries the sound of the telephone in that room

and traffic far off and doves under the window
chuckling coolly and his voice saying,
You beauty. I can feel that beauty's

heart beating inside mine as she presses into his arms in the high blue room—
No, I say aloud. I force my arms down
through air which is suddenly cold and heavy as water

and the videotape jerks to a halt
like a glass slide under a drop of blood.
I stop and turn and stand into the wind,

which now plunges towards me over the moor.
When Law left I felt so bad I thought I would die.
This is not uncommon.

I took up the practice of meditation.
Each morning I sat on the floor in front of my sofa
and chanted bits of old Latin prayers.

De profundis clamavi ad te Domine.
Each morning a vision came to me.
Gradually I understood that these were naked glimpses of my soul.

I called them Nudes.
Nude #1. Woman alone on a hill.
She stands into the wind.

It is a hard wind slanting from the north.
Long flaps and shreds of flesh rip off the woman's body and lift
and blow away on the wind, leaving

an exposed column of nerve and blood and muscle
calling mutely through lipless mouth.
It pains me to record this,

I am not a melodramatic person.
But soul is "hewn in a wild workshop"
as Charlotte Brontë says of *Wuthering Heights.*

Charlotte's preface to *Wuthering Heights* is a publicist's masterpiece.
Like someone carefully not looking at a scorpion
crouched on the arm of the sofa Charlotte

talks firmly and calmly
about the other furniture of Emily's workshop—about
the inexorable spirit ("stronger than a man, simpler than a child"),

the cruel illness ("pain no words can render"),
the autonomous end ("she sank rapidly, she made haste to leave us")
and about Emily's total subjection

to a creative project she could neither understand nor control,
and for which she deserves no more praise nor blame
than if she had opened her mouth

"to breathe lightning." The scorpion is inching down
the arm of the sofa while Charlotte
continues to speak helpfully about lightning

and other weather we may expect to experience
when we enter Emily's electrical atmosphere.
It is "a horror of great darkness" that awaits us there

but Emily is not responsible. Emily was in the grip.
"Having formed these beings she did not know what she had done,"
says Charlotte (of Heathcliff and Earnshaw and Catherine).

Well there are many ways of being held prisoner.
The scorpion takes a light spring and lands on our left knee
as Charlotte concludes, "On herself she had no pity."

Pitiless too are the Heights, which Emily called Wuthering
because of their "bracing ventilation"
and "a north wind over the edge."

Whaching a north wind grind the moor
that surrounded her father's house on every side,
formed of a kind of rock called millstone grit,

taught Emily all she knew about love and its necessities—
an angry education that shapes the way her characters
use one another. "My love for Heathcliff," says Catherine,

"resembles the eternal rocks beneath—
a source of little visible delight, but necessary."
Necessary? I notice the sun has dimmed

and the afternoon air sharpening.
I turn and start to recross the moor towards home.
What are the imperatives

that hold people like Catherine and Heathcliff
together and apart, like pores blown into hot rock
and then stranded out of reach

of one another when it hardens? What kind of necessity is that?
The last time I saw Law was a black night in September.
Autumn had begun,

my knees were cold inside my clothes.
A chill fragment of moon rose.
He stood in my living room and spoke

without looking at me. Not enough spin on it,
he said of our five years of love.
Inside my chest I felt my heart snap into two pieces

which floated apart. By now I was so cold
it was like burning. I put out my hand
to touch his. He moved back.

I don't want to be sexual with you, he said. Everything gets crazy.
But now he was looking at me.
Yes, I said as I began to remove my clothes.

Everything gets crazy. When nude
I turned my back because he likes the back.
He moved onto me.

Everything I know about love and its necessities
I learned in that one moment
when I found myself

thrusting my little burning red backside like a baboon
at a man who no longer cherished me.
There was no area of my mind

not appalled by this action, no part of my body
that could have done otherwise.
But to talk of mind and body begs the question.

Soul is the place,
stretched like a surface of millstone grit between body and mind,
where such necessity grinds itself out.

Soul is what I kept watch on all that night.
Law stayed with me.
We lay on top of the covers as if it weren't really a night of sleep and
time,

caressing and singing to one another in our made-up language
like the children we used to be.
That was a night that centred Heaven and Hell,

as Emily would say. We tried to fuck
but he remained limp, although happy. I came
again and again, each time accumulating lucidity,

until at last I was floating high up near the ceiling looking down
on the two souls clasped there on the bed
with their mortal boundaries

visible around them like lines on a map.
I saw the lines harden.
He left in the morning.

It is very cold
walking into the long scraped April wind.
At this time of year there is no sunset
just some movements inside the light and then a sinking away.

KITCHEN

Kitchen is quiet as a bone when I come in.
No sound from the rest of the house.
I wait a moment
then open the fridge.

Brilliant as a spaceship it exhales cold confusion.
My mother lives alone and eats little but her fridge is always crammed.
After extracting the yogurt container

from beneath a wily arrangement of leftover blocks of Christmas cake
wrapped in foil and prescription medicine bottles
I close the fridge door. Bluish dusk

fills the room like a sea slid back.
I lean against the sink.
White foods taste best to me

and I prefer to eat alone. I don't know why.
Once I heard girls singing a May Day song that went:

> Violante in the pantry
> Gnawing at a mutton bone
> How she gnawed it
> How she clawed it
> When she felt herself alone.

Girls are cruelest to themselves.
Someone like Emily Brontë,
who remained a girl all her life despite her body as a woman,

had cruelty drifted up in all the cracks of her like spring snow.
We can see her ridding herself of it at various times
with a gesture like she used to brush the carpet.

Reason with him and then whip him!
was her instruction (age six) to her father
regarding brother Branwell.

And when she was 14 and bitten by a rabid dog she strode (they say)
into the kitchen and taking red hot tongs from the back of the stove
    applied
them directly to her arm.

Cauterization of Heathcliff took longer.
More than thirty years in the time of the novel,
from the April evening when he runs out the back door of the kitchen
and vanishes over the moor

because he overheard half a sentence of Catherine's
("It would degrade me to marry Heathcliff")
until the wild morning

when the servant finds him stark dead and grinning
on his rainsoaked bed upstairs in Wuthering Heights.
Heathcliff is a pain devil.

If he had stayed in the kitchen
long enough to hear the other half of Catherine's sentence
("so he will never know how I love him")

Heathcliff would have been set free.
But Emily knew how to catch a devil.
She put into him in place of a soul

the constant cold departure of Catherine from his nervous system
every time he drew a breath or moved thought.
She broke all his moments in half,

with the kitchen door standing open.
I am not unfamiliar with this half-life.
But there is more to it than that.

Heathcliff's sexual despair
arose out of no such experience in the life of Emily Brontë,
so far as we know. Her question,

which concerns the years of inner cruelty that can twist a person into
a pain devil,
came to her in a kindly firelit kitchen
("kichin" in Emily's spelling) where she

and Charlotte and Anne peeled potatoes together
and made up stories with the old house dog Keeper at their feet.
There is a fragment

of a poem she wrote in 1839
(about six years before *Wuthering Heights*) that says:

> That iron man was born like me
> And he was once an ardent boy:
> He must have felt in infancy
> The glory of a summer sky.

Who is the iron man?
My mother's voice cuts across me,
from the next room where she is lying on the sofa.

Is that you dear?
Yes Ma.
Why don't you turn on a light in there?

Out the kitchen window I watch the steely April sun
jab its last cold yellow streaks
across a dirty silver sky.
Okay Ma. What's for supper?

LIBERTY

Liberty means different things to different people.
I have never liked lying in bed in the morning.
Law did.
My mother does.

But as soon as the morning light hits my eyes I want to be out in it—
moving along the moor
into the first blue currents and cold navigation of everything awake.

I hear my mother in the next room turn and sigh and sink deeper.
I peel the stale cage of sheets off my legs
and I am free.

Out on the moor all is brilliant and hard after a night of frost.
The light plunges straight up from the ice to a blue hole at the top of the sky.
Frozen mud crunches underfoot. The sound

startles me back into the dream I was having
this morning when I awoke,
one of those nightlong sweet dreams of lying in Law's

arms like a needle in water—it is a physical effort
to pull myself out of his white silk hands
as they slide down my dream hips—I

turn and face into the wind
and begin to run.
Goblins, devils and death stream behind me.

In the days and months after Law left
I felt as if the sky was torn off my life.
I had no home in goodness anymore.

To see the love between Law and me
turn into two animals gnawing and craving through one another
towards some other hunger was terrible.

Perhaps this is what people mean by original sin, I thought.
But what love could be prior to it?
What is prior?

What is love?
My questions were not original.
Nor did I answer them.

Mornings when I meditated
I was presented with a nude glimpse of my lone soul,
not the complex mysteries of love and hate.

But the Nudes are still as clear in my mind
as pieces of laundry that froze on the clothesline overnight.
There were in all thirteen of them.

Nude #2. Woman caught in a cage of thorns.
Big glistening brown thorns with black stains on them
where she twists this way and that way

unable to stand upright.
Nude #3. Woman with a single great thorn implanted in her forehead.
She grips it in both hands

endeavouring to wrench it out.
Nude #4. Woman on a blasted landscape
backlit in red like Hieronymus Bosch.

Covering her head and upper body is a hellish contraption
like the top half of a crab.
With arms crossed as if pulling off a sweater

she works hard at dislodging the crab.
It was about this time
I began telling Dr. Haw

about the Nudes. She said,
When you see these horrible images why do you stay with them?
Why keep watching? Why not

go away? I was amazed.
Go away where? I said.
This still seems to me a good question.

But by now the day is wide open and a strange young April light
is filling the moor with gold milk.
I have reached the middle

where the ground goes down into a depression and fills with swampy
    water.
It is frozen.
A solid black pane of moor life caught in its own night attitudes.

Certain wild gold arrangements of weed are visible deep in the black.
Four naked alder trunks rise straight up from it
and sway in the blue air. Each trunk

where it enters the ice radiates a map of silver pressures—
thousands of hair-thin cracks catching the white of the light
like a jailed face

catching grins through the bars.
Emily Brontë has a poem about a woman in jail who says

> A messenger of Hope, comes every night to me
> And offers, for short life, eternal Liberty.

I wonder what kind of Liberty this is.
Her critics and commentators say she means death
or a visionary experience that prefigures death.

They understand her prison
as the limitations placed on a clergyman's daughter
by nineteenth-century life in a remote parish on a cold moor

in the north of England.
They grow impatient with the extreme terms in which she figures
prison life.
"In so much of Brontë's work

the self-dramatising and posturing of these poems teeters
on the brink of a potentially bathetic melodrama,"
says one. Another

refers to "the cardboard sublime" of her caught world.
I stopped telling my psychotherapist about the Nudes
when I realized I had no way to answer her question,

Why keep watching?
Some people watch, that's all I can say.
There is nowhere else to go,

no ledge to climb up to.
Perhaps I can explain this to her if I wait for the right moment,
as with a very difficult sister.

"On that mind time and experience alone could work:
to the influence of other intellects it was not amenable,"
wrote Charlotte of Emily.

I wonder what kind of conversation these two had
over breakfast at the parsonage.
"My sister Emily

was not a person of demonstrative character," Charlotte emphasizes,
"nor one on the recesses of whose mind and feelings,
even those nearest and dearest to her could,

with impunity, intrude unlicensed. . . ." Recesses were many.
One autumn day in 1845 Charlotte
"accidentally lighted on a MS. volume of verse in my sister Emily's
handwriting."

It was a small (4 × 6) notebook
with a dark red cover marked 6d.
and contained 44 poems in Emily's minute hand.

Charlotte had known Emily wrote verse
but felt "more than surprise" at its quality.
"Not at all like the poetry women generally write."

Further surprise awaited Charlotte when she read Emily's novel,
not least for its foul language.
She gently probes this recess

in her Editor's Preface to *Wuthering Heights*.
"A large class of readers, likewise, will suffer greatly
from the introduction into the pages of this work

of words printed with all their letters,
which it has become the custom to represent by the initial and final
letter only—a blank
line filling the interval."

Well, there are different definitions of Liberty.
Love is freedom, Law was fond of saying.
I took this to be more a wish than a thought

and changed the subject.
But blank lines do not say nothing.
As Charlotte puts it,

"The practice of hinting by single letters those expletives
with which profane and violent persons are wont to garnish their
discourse,
strikes me as a proceeding which,

however well meant, is weak and futile.
I cannot tell what good it does—what feeling it spares—
what horror it conceals."

I turn my steps and begin walking back over the moor
towards home and breakfast.
It is a two-way traffic,

the language of the unsaid. My favourite pages
of *The Collected Works Of Emily Brontë*
are the notes at the back

recording small adjustments made by Charlotte
to the text of Emily's verse,
which Charlotte edited for publication after Emily's death.
"*Prison* for *strongest* [in Emily's hand] altered to *lordly* by Charlotte."

HERO

I can tell by the way my mother chews her toast
whether she had a good night
and is about to say a happy thing
or not.

Not.
She puts her toast down on the side of her plate.
You know you can pull the drapes in that room, she begins.

This is a coded reference to one of our oldest arguments,
from what I call The Rules Of Life series.
My mother always closes her bedroom drapes tight before going to
bed at night.

I open mine as wide as possible.
I like to see everything, I say.
What's there to see?

Moon. Air. Sunrise.
All that light on your face in the morning. Wakes you up.
I like to wake up.

At this point the drapes argument has reached a delta
and may advance along one of three channels.
There is the What You Need Is A Good Night's Sleep channel,

the Stubborn As Your Father channel
and random channel.
More toast? I interpose strongly, pushing back my chair.

Those women! says my mother with an exasperated rasp.
Mother has chosen random channel.
Women?

Complaining about rape all the time—
I see she is tapping one furious finger on yesterday's newspaper
lying beside the grape jam.

The front page has a small feature
about a rally for International Women's Day—
have you had a look at the Sears Summer Catalogue?

Nope.
Why, it's a disgrace! Those bathing suits—
cut way up to here! (she points) No wonder!

You're saying women deserve to get raped
because Sears bathing suit ads
have high-cut legs? Ma, are you serious?

Well someone has to be responsible.
Why should women be responsible for male desire? My voice is high.
Oh I see you're one of Them.

One of Whom? My voice is very high. Mother vaults it.
And whatever did you do with that little tank suit you had last year
    the green one?
It looked so smart on you.

The frail fact drops on me from a great height
that my mother is afraid.
She will be eighty years old this summer.

Her tiny sharp shoulders hunched in the blue bathrobe
make me think of Emily Brontë's little merlin hawk Hero
that she fed bits of bacon at the kitchen table when Charlotte wasn't
    around.

So Ma, we'll go—I pop up the toaster
and toss a hot slice of pumpernickel lightly across onto her plate—
visit Dad today? She eyes the kitchen clock with hostility.

Leave at eleven, home again by four? I continue.
She is buttering her toast with jagged strokes.
Silence is assent in our code. I go into the next room to phone the
    taxi.

My father lives in a hospital for patients who need chronic care
about 50 miles from here.
He suffers from a kind of dementia

characterized by two sorts of pathological change
first recorded in 1907 by Alois Alzheimer.
First, the presence in cerebral tissue

of a spherical formation known as neuritic plaque,
consisting mainly of degenerating brain cells.
Second, neurofibrillary snarlings

in the cerebral cortex and in the hippocampus.
There is no known cause or cure.
Mother visits him by taxi once a week

for the last five years.
Marriage is for better or for worse, she says,
this is the worse.

So about an hour later we are in the taxi
shooting along empty country roads towards town.
The April light is clear as an alarm.

As we pass them it gives a sudden sense of every object
existing in space on its own shadow.
I wish I could carry this clarity with me

into the hospital where distinctions tend to flatten and coalesce.
I wish I had been nicer to him before he got crazy.
These are my two wishes.

It is hard to find the beginning of dementia.
I remember a night about ten years ago
when I was talking to him on the telephone.

It was a Sunday night in winter.
I heard his sentences filling up with fear.
He would start a sentence—about weather, lose his way, start another.
It made me furious to hear him floundering—

my tall proud father, former World War II navigator!
It made me merciless.
I stood on the edge of the conversation,

watching him thrash about for cues,
offering none,
and it came to me like a slow avalanche

that he had no idea who he was talking to.
Much colder today I guess. . . .
his voice pressed into the silence and broke off,

snow falling on it.
There was a long pause while snow covered us both.
Well I won't keep you,

he said with sudden desperate cheer as if sighting land.
I'll say goodnight now,
I won't run up your bill. Goodbye.

Goodbye.
Goodbye. Who are you?
I said into the dial tone.

At the hospital we pass down long pink halls
through a door with a big window
and a combination lock (5–25–3)

to the west wing, for chronic care patients.
Each wing has a name.
The chronic wing is Our Golden Mile

although mother prefers to call it The Last Lap.
Father sits strapped in a chair which is tied to the wall
in a room of other tied people tilting at various angles.

My father tilts least, I am proud of him.
Hi Dad how y'doing?
His face cracks open it could be a grin or rage

and looking past me he issues a stream of vehemence at the air.
My mother lays her hand on his.
Hello love, she says. He jerks his hand away. We sit.

Sunlight flocks through the room.
Mother begins to unpack from her handbag the things she has brought for him,
grapes, arrowroot biscuits, humbugs.

He is addressing strenuous remarks to someone in the air between us.
He uses a language known only to himself,
made of snarls and syllables and sudden wild appeals.

Once in a while some old formula floats up through the wash—
You don't say! or Happy birthday to you!—
but no real sentence

for more than three years now.
I notice his front teeth are getting black.
I wonder how you clean the teeth of mad people.

He always took good care of his teeth. My mother looks up.
She and I often think two halves of one thought.
Do you remember that gold-plated toothpick

you sent him from Harrod's the summer you were in London? she asks.
Yes I wonder what happened to it.
Must be in the bathroom somewhere.

She is giving him grapes one by one.
They keep rolling out of his huge stiff fingers.
He used to be a big man, over six feet tall and strong,

but since he came to hospital his body has shrunk to the merest bone house—
except the hands. The hands keep growing.
Each one now as big as a boot in Van Gogh,

they go lumbering after the grapes in his lap.
But now he turns to me with a rush of urgent syllables
that break off on a high note—he waits,

staring into my face. That quizzical look.
One eyebrow at an angle.
I have a photograph taped to my fridge at home.

It shows his World War II air crew posing in front of the plane.
Hands firmly behind backs, legs wide apart,
chins forward.

Dressed in the puffed flying suits
with a wide leather strap pulled tight through the crotch.
They squint into the brilliant winter sun of 1942.

It is dawn.
They are leaving Dover for France.
My father on the far left is the tallest airman,

with his collar up,
one eyebrow at an angle.
The shadowless light makes him look immortal,

for all the world like someone who will not weep again.
He is still staring into my face.
Flaps down! I cry.
His black grin flares once and goes out like a match.

HOT

Hot blue moonlight down the steep sky.
I wake too fast from a cellar of hanged puppies
with my eyes pouring into the dark.
Fumbling

and slowly
consciousness replaces the bars.
Dreamtails and angry liquids

swim back down to the middle of me.
It is generally anger dreams that occupy my nights now.
This is not uncommon after loss of love—

blue and black and red blasting the crater open.
I am interested in anger.
I clamber along to find the source.

My dream was of an old woman lying awake in bed.
She controls the house by a system of light bulbs strung above her on wires.
Each wire has a little black switch.

One by one the switches refuse to turn the bulbs on.
She keeps switching and switching
in rising tides of very hot anger.

Then she creeps out of bed to peer through lattices
at the rooms of the rest of the house.
The rooms are silent and brilliantly lit

and full of huge furniture beneath which crouch
small creatures—not quite cats not quite rats
licking their narrow red jaws

under a load of time.
I want to be beautiful again, she whispers
but the great overlit rooms tick emptily

as a deserted oceanliner and now behind her in the dark
a rustling sound, comes—
My pajamas are soaked.

Anger travels through me, pushes aside everything else in my heart,
pouring up the vents.
Every night I wake to this anger,

the soaked bed,
the hot pain box slamming me each way I move.
I want justice. Slam.

I want an explanation. Slam.
I want to curse the false friend who said I love you forever. Slam.
I reach up and switch on the bedside lamp. Night springs

out the window and is gone over the moor.
I lie listening to the light vibrate in my ears
and thinking about curses.

Emily Brontë was good at cursing.
Falsity and bad love and the deadly pain of alteration are constant
topics in her verse.

> Well, thou hast paid me back my love!
> But if there be a God above
> Whose arm is strong, whose word is true,
> This hell shall wring thy spirit too!

The curses are elaborate:

> There go, Deceiver, go! My hand is streaming wet;
> My heart's blood flows to buy the blessing—To forget!
> Oh could that lost heart give back, back again to thine,
> One tenth part of the pain that clouds my dark decline!

But they do not bring her peace:

> Vain words, vain frenzied thoughts! No ear can hear me call—
> Lost in the vacant air my frantic curses fall. . . .
>
> Unconquered in my soul the Tyrant rules me still—
> *Life* bows to my control, but *Love* I cannot kill!

Her anger is a puzzle.
It raises many questions in me,
to see love treated with such cold and knowing contempt

by someone who rarely left home
"except to go to church or take a walk on the hills"
(Charlotte tells us) and who

had no more intercourse with Haworth folk
than "a nun has
of the country people who sometimes pass her convent gates."

How did Emily come to lose faith in humans?
She admired their dialects, studied their genealogies,
"but with them she rarely exchanged a word."

Her introvert nature shrank from shaking hands with someone she met on the moor.
What did Emily know of lover's lies or cursive human faith?
Among her biographers

is one who conjectures she bore or aborted a child
during her six-month stay in Halifax,
but there is no evidence at all for such an event

and the more general consensus is that Emily did not touch a man in her 31 years.
Banal sexism aside,
I find myself tempted

to read *Wuthering Heights* as one thick stacked act of revenge
for all that life withheld from Emily.
But the poetry shows traces of a deeper explanation.

As if anger could be a kind of vocation for some women.
It is a chilly thought.

> The heart is dead since infancy.
> Unwept for let the body go.

Suddenly cold I reach down and pull the blanket back up to my chin.
The vocation of anger is not mine.
I know my source.

It is stunning, it is a moment like no other,
when one's lover comes in and says I do not love you anymore.
I switch off the lamp and lie on my back,

thinking about Emily's cold young soul.
Where does unbelief begin?
When I was young

there were degrees of certainty.
I could say, Yes I know that I have two hands.
Then one day I awakened on a planet of people whose hands
occasionally disappear—

From the next room I hear my mother shift and sigh and settle
back down under the doorsill of sleep.
Out the window the moon is just a cold bit of silver gristle low on
fading banks of sky.

> Our guests are darkly lodged, I whispered, gazing through
> The vault . . .

THOU

The question I am left with is the question of her loneliness.
And I prefer to put it off.
It is morning.

Astonished light is washing over the moor from north to east.
I am walking into the light.
One way to put off loneliness is to interpose God.

Emily had a relationship on this level with someone she calls Thou.
She describes Thou as awake like herself all night
and full of strange power.

Thou woos Emily with a voice that comes out of the night wind.
Thou and Emily influence one another in the darkness,
playing near and far at once.

She talks about a sweetness that "proved us one."
I am uneasy with the compensatory model of female religious
experience and yet,
there is no question,

it would be sweet to have a friend to tell things to at night,
without the terrible sex price to pay.
This is a childish idea, I know.

My education, I have to admit, has been gappy.
The basic rules of male-female relations
were imparted atmospherically in our family,

no direct speech allowed.
I remember one Sunday I was sitting in the backseat of the car.
Father in front.

We were waiting in the driveway for mother,
who came around the corner of the house
and got into the passenger side of the car

dressed in a yellow Chanel suit and black high heels.
Father glanced sideways at her.
Showing a good bit of leg today Mother, he said

in a voice which I (age eleven) thought odd.
I stared at the back of her head waiting for what she would say.
Her answer would clear this up.

But she just laughed a strange laugh with ropes all over it.
Later that summer I put this laugh together with another laugh
I overheard as I was going upstairs.

She was talking on the telephone in the kitchen.
Well a woman would be just as happy with a kiss on the cheek
most of the time but YOU KNOW MEN,

she was saying. Laugh.
Not ropes, thorns.
I have arrived at the middle of the moor

where the ground goes down into a low swampy place.
The swamp water is frozen solid.
Bits of gold weed

have etched themselves
on the underside of the ice like messages.

> I'll come when thou art saddest,
> Laid alone in the darkened room;
> When the mad day's mirth has vanished,
> And the smile of joy is banished,
>
> I'll come when the heart's real feeling
> Has entire, unbiased sway,
> And my influence o'er thee stealing
> Grief deepening, joy congealing,
> Shall bear thy soul away.
>
> Listen! 'tis just the hour,
> The awful time for thee:
> Dost thou not feel upon thy soul
> A flood of strange sensations roll,
> Forerunners of a sterner power,
> Heralds of me?

Very hard to read, the messages that pass
between Thou and Emily.
In this poem she reverses their roles,

speaking not *as* the victim but *to* the victim.
It is chilling to watch Thou move upon thou,
who lies alone in the dark waiting to be mastered.

It is a shock to realize that this low, slow collusion
of master and victim within one voice
is a rationale

for the most awful loneliness of the poet's hour.
She has reversed the roles of thou and Thou
not as a display of power

but to force out of herself some pity
for this soul trapped in glass,
which is her true creation.

Those nights lying alone
are not discontinuous with this cold hectic dawn.
It is who I am.

Is it a vocation of anger?
Why construe silence
as the Real Presence?

Why stoop to kiss this doorstep?
Why be unstrung and pounded flat and pine away
imagining someone vast to whom I may vent the swell of my soul?

Emily was fond of Psalm 130.
"My soul waiteth on Thou more than they that watch for the morning,
I say more than they that watch for the morning."

I like to believe that for her the act of watching provided a shelter,
that her collusion with Thou gave ease to anger and desire:
"In Thou they are quenched as a fire of thorns," says the psalmist.

But for myself I do not believe this, I am not quenched—
with Thou or without Thou I find no shelter.
I am my own Nude.

And Nudes have a difficult sexual destiny.
I have watched this destiny disclose itself
in its jerky passage from girl to woman to who I am now,

from love to anger to this cold marrow,
from fire to shelter to fire.
What is the opposite of believing in Thou—

merely not believing in Thou? No. That is too simple.
That is to prepare a misunderstanding.
I want to speak more clearly.

Perhaps the Nudes are the best way.
Nude #5. Deck of cards.
Each card is made of flesh.

The living cards are days of a woman's life.
I see a great silver needle go flashing right through the deck once
from end to end.
Nude #6 I cannot remember.

Nude #7. White room whose walls,
having neither planes nor curves nor angles,
are composed of a continuous satiny white membrane

like the flesh of some interior organ of the moon.
It is a living surface, almost wet.
Lucency breathes in and out.

Rainbows shudder across it.
And around the walls of the room a voice goes whispering,
Be very careful. Be very careful.

Nude #8. Black disc on which the fires of all the winds
are attached in a row.
A woman stands on the disc

amid the winds whose long yellow silk flames
flow and vibrate up through her.
Nude #9. Transparent loam.

Under the loam a woman has dug a long deep trench.
Into the trench she is placing small white forms, I don't know what they are.
Nude #10. Green thorn of the world poking up

alive through the heart of a woman
who lies on her back on the ground.
The thorn is exploding

its green blood above her in the air.
Everything it is it has, the voice says.
Nude #11. Ledge in outer space.

Space is bluish black and glossy as solid water
and moving very fast in all directions,
shrieking past the woman who stands pinned

to nothing by its pressure.
She peers and glances for some way to go, trying to lift her hand but cannot.
Nude #12. Old pole in the wind.

Cold currents are streaming over it
and pulling out
into ragged long horizontal black lines

some shreds of ribbon
attached to the pole.
I cannot see how they are attached—

notches? staples? nails? All of a sudden the wind changes
and all the black shreds rise straight up in the air
and tie themselves into knots,

then untie and float down.
The wind is gone.
It waits.

By this time, midway through winter,
I had become entirely fascinated with my spiritual melodrama.
Then it stopped.

Days passed, months passed and I saw nothing.
I continued to peer and glance, sitting on the rug in front of my sofa
in the curtainless morning

with my nerves open to the air like something skinned.
I saw nothing.
Outside the window spring storms came and went.

April snow folded its huge white paws over doors and porches.
I watched a chunk of it lean over the roof and break off
and fall and I thought,

How slow! as it glided soundlessly past,
but still—nothing. No nudes.
No Thou.

A great icicle formed on the railing of my balcony
so I drew up close to the window and tried peering through the
icicle,
hoping to trick myself into some interior vision,

but all I saw
was the man and woman in the room across the street
making their bed and laughing.

I stopped watching.
I forgot about Nudes.
I lived my life,

which felt like a switched-off TV.
Something had gone through me and out and I could not own it.
"No need now to tremble for the hard frost and the keen wind.

Emily does not feel them,"
wrote Charlotte the day after burying her sister.
Emily had shaken free.

A soul can do that.
Whether it goes to join Thou and sit on the porch for all eternity
enjoying jokes and kisses and beautiful cold spring evenings,

you and I will never know. But I can tell you what I saw.
Nude #13 arrived when I was not watching for it.
It came at night.

Very much like Nude #1.
And yet utterly different.
I saw a high hill and on it a form shaped against hard air.

It could have been just a pole with some old cloth attached,
but as I came closer
I saw it was a human body

trying to stand against winds so terrible that the flesh was blowing off the bones.
And there was no pain.
The wind

was cleansing the bones.
They stood forth silver and necessary.
It was not my body, not a woman's body, it was the body of us all.
It walked out of the light.

THE TRUTH ABOUT GOD

My Religion

My religion makes no sense
and does not help me
therefore I pursue it.

When we see
how simple it would have been
we will thrash ourselves.

I had a vision
of all the people in the world
who are searching for God

massed in a room
on one side
of a partition

that looks
from the other side
(God's side)

transparent
but we are blind.
Our gestures are blind.

Our blind gestures continue
for some time until finally
from somewhere

on the other side of the partition there we are
looking back at them.
It is far too late.

We see how brokenly
how warily
how ill

our blind gestures
parodied
what God really wanted

(some simple thing).
The thought of it
(this simple thing)

is like a creature
let loose in a room
and battering

to get out.
It batters my soul
with its rifle butt.

The God Fit

Sometimes God will drop a fit on you.
Leave you on your bed howling.
Don't take it meanly.

Because the outer walls of God are glass.
I see a million souls clambering up the walls on the inside
to escape God who is burning,

untended.

The God Coup

God is a grand heart cut.
On the road where man surges along He may,
as the prophet says,
tarry.

By God

Sometimes by night I don't know why
I awake thinking of prepositions.
Perhaps they are clues.

"Since by Man came Death."
I am puzzled to hear that Man is the agent of Death.
Perhaps it means

Man was standing at the curb
and Death came by.
Once I had a dog

would go with anyone.
Perhaps listening for
little by little the first union.

Deflect

I have a friend who is red hot with pain.
He feels the lights like hard rain through his pores.
Together we went to ask Isaac.

Isaac said I will tell you the story told to me.
It was from Adam
issued the lights.

From the lights of his forehead were formed all the names of the world.
From the lights of his ears, nose and throat
came a function no one has ever defined.

From the lights of his eyes—but wait—
Isaac waits.
In theory

the lights of the eye should have issued from Adam's navel.
But within the lights themselves occurred
an intake of breath

and they changed their path.
And they were separated.
And they were caught in the head.

And from these separated lights came
that which pains you
on its errands (here my friend began to weep) through the world.

For be assured it is not only you who mourn.
Isaac lashed his tail.
Every rank of world

was caused to descend
(at least one rank)
by the terrible pressure of the light.

Nothing remained in place.
Nothing was not captured except
among the shards and roots and matter

some lights
from Adam's eyes
nourished there somehow.

Isaac stopped his roaring.
And my friend by now drowsy as a snake
subsided behind a heap of blueblack syllables.

God's Name

God had no name.
Isaac had two names.
Isaac was also called The Blind.

Inside the dark sky of his mind
Isaac could hear God
moving down a country road bordered by trees.

By the way the trees reflected off God
Isaac knew which ones were straight and tall
or when they carried their branches

as a body does its head
or why some crouched low to the ground in thickets.
To hear how God was moving through the universe

gave Isaac his question.
I could tell you his answer
but it wouldn't help.

The name is not a noun.
It is an adverb.
Like the little black notebooks that Beethoven carried

in his coatpocket
for the use of those who wished to converse with him,
the God adverb

is a one-way street that goes everywhere you are.
No use telling you what it is.
Just chew it and rub it on.

Teresa Of God

"the aching has hold of me O grievous daimon"

Teresa lived in a personal black cube.
I saw her hit the wall each way she moved.
She cursed her heart

which was, she said, rent
and her nose
which had been broken again and again.

Some people have to fight every moment of their lives
which God has lined with a burning animal—
I think because

God wants that animal kept alive.
With her nose Teresa questioned
this project of God's.

To her heart God sent answer.
The autopsy after her death revealed
it was indeed rent.

Photographs of the event
had to be faked (with red thread and an old gold glove)
when the lens kept melting.

The Grace That Comes By Violence

Yours is not (I regret to say) the story they tell
although you howl and gash yourself
scurrying out of the tombs

where you now live.
God forces some.
God's prophet came

to send your unclean spirit
into pigs, who ran amok.
I saw you

at the bottom of the cliff of pity
diving in pig blood—
"cleansed" now.

God's Woman

Are you angry at nature? said God to His woman.
Yes I am angry at nature I do not want nature stuck
up between my legs on your pink baton

or ladled out like geography whenever
your buckle needs a lick.
What do you mean *Creation*?

God circled her.
Fire. Time. Fire.
Choose, said God.

God Stiff

God gave an onomatopoeic quality to women's language.
These eternally blundering sounds eternally
blundering down

into the real words of what they are
like feet dropped into bone shoes.
"Treachery" (she notices) sounds just like His zipper going down.

God's Beloveds Remain True

Chaos overshadows us.
Unsheltered sorrow shuts upon us.
We are strangled by bitter light.
Our bones shake like sticks.
We snap.
We grope.
We pant and go dry.
Our tongues are black.
All day is endless.
Nights endless.
Our skin crawls, it cracks.
Our room is a cat who plays with us.
Our hope is a noose.
We take our flesh in our teeth.
The autumn blows us as chaff across the fields.
We are sifted and fall.
We are hung in a void.
We are shattered on the ocean.
We are smeared on the darkness.
We are slit and drained out.
Little things drink us.
We lie unburied.
We are dust.
We know nothing.
We can not answer.
We will speak no more.
BUT WE WILL NOT STOP.
For we are the beloveds.
We have been instructed to call this His love.

God's Bouquet Of Undying Love

April snow.
God is waiting in the garden.
Slow as a blush,

snow shifts and settles on God.
On God's bouquet.
The trees are white nerve nets.

God's Mother

She doesn't get to say much in the official biography—
I believe they are out of wine, etc.,
practical things—

watching with one eye as he goes about the world
calling himself The Son Of Man.
Naturalists tell us

that the hatching crow is fed by the male
but when it flies, by the mother.

Love	Fly	Man
Loves	Flies	Mans
Loved	Flew	Manned
Loving	Flying	Manning
Loved	Flown	Woman.

It is what grammarians call a difference of tense and aspect.

God's Justice

In the beginning there were days set aside for various tasks.
On the day He was to create justice
God got involved in making a dragonfly

and lost track of time.
It was about two inches long
with turquoise dots all down its back like Lauren Bacall.

God watched it bend its tiny wire elbows
as it set about cleaning the transparent case of its head.
The eye globes mounted on the case

rotated this way and that
as it polished every angle.
Inside the case

which was glassy black like the windows of a downtown bank
God could see the machinery humming
and He watched the hum

travel all the way down turquoise dots to the end of the tail
and breathe off as light.
Its black wings vibrated in and out.

The Wolf God

Like a painting we will be erased, no one can remain.
I saw my life as a wolf loping along the road
and I questioned the women of that place.

Some regard the wolf as immortal, they said.
Now you know this only happened in one case and that
wolves die regularly of various causes—

bears kill them, tigers hunt them,
they get epilepsy,
they get a salmon bone crosswise in their throat,

they run themselves to death no one knows why—
but perhaps you never heard
of their ear trouble.

They have very good ears,
can hear a cloud pass overhead.
And sometimes it happens

that a windblown seed will bury itself in the aural canal
displacing equilibrium.
They go mad trying to stand upright,

nothing to link with.
Die of anger.
Only one we know learned to go along with it.

He took small steps at first.
Using the updrafts.
They called him Huizkol,

that means
Looks Good In Spring.
Things are as hard as you make them.

God's Christ Theory

God had no emotions but wished temporarily
to move in man's mind
as if He did: Christ.

Not passion but compassion.
Com—means "with."
What kind of withness would that be?

Translate it.
I have a friend named Jesus
from Mexico.

His father and grandfather are called Jesus too.
They account me a fool with my questions about salvation.
They say they are saving to move to Los Angeles.

God's List Of Liquids

It was a November night of wind.
Leaves tore past the window.
God had the book of life open at PLEASURE

and was holding the pages down with one hand
because of the wind from the door.
For I made their flesh as a sieve

wrote God at the top of the page
and then listed in order:
Alcohol
Blood
Gratitude
Memory
Semen
Song
Tears
Time.

God's Work

Moonlight in the kitchen is a sign of God.
The kind of sadness that is a black suction pipe extracting you
from your own navel and which the Buddhists call

"no mindcover" is a sign of God.
The blind alleys that run alongside human conversation
like lashes are a sign of God.

God's own calmness is a sign of God.
The surprisingly cold smell of potatoes or money.
Solid pieces of silence.

From these diverse signs you can see
how much work remains to do.
Put away your sadness, it is a mantle of work.

TV MEN

TV Men: Hektor

I.

TV is hardhearted, like Lenin.
TV is rational, like mowing.
TV is wrong, often, a worry.
TV is ugly, like the future.
TV is a classic example.

Hektor's family members found themselves engaged in exciting acts,
and using excited language, which they knew derived from TV.

A classic example of what.

A classic example of a strain of cruelty.

II.

Hektor was born to be a prince of Troy not a man of TV,
hence his success.
Wrong people look good on TV, they are so obviously
a soul divided

and we all enjoy the pathos of that.
Let us join Hektor
on the eve of the Death Valley shoot.
Hektor lies

on the motel bed in his armour observing himself and his red lips
high overhead.
The ceiling is mirrored in divine fire.
Your Law has got hold

of my entrails, he murmurs. His lipstick grins at him
upside down.
Out the window he can see a horizon of low brown mountains
laid end to end.

They make a hissing sound. O prince of Troy!
Butter and honey
shall you eat, that you may know to refuse the evil
and choose the good.

TV is inherently cynical. It speaks to the eye, but the mind has no eye.

III.

Hektor's name is from the ancient verb "to hold."
Hold.
Hold on.
Hold out.
Hold up.
Hold off.
Hold in.
Hold together.
Hektor's name is the antithesis
of those temporary constructions on the shore
(Greek army)
that
stood—
from opening kills to the day Troy was razed—
a mere ten years.

Head down against a thin winter wind
Hektor paces the floor of Death Valley,
repeating his line.
I have learned to be brave.
The light-hole pulls away on every side.

TV is dull, like the block of self in each of us.

IV.

Salt particle by salt particle the desert grows luminous at dawn.
It is the second day of the Death Valley shoot.
Hektor is alone in the light-hole.

The walkie-talkie taped to the small of his back is cold as a slab of
meat.
It crackles alive and the director's voice
crawls up his spine like a bee.

Places please! Helicopter five minutes away!
Hektor hunkers down close to the sand.
The eunuch winter sun

stains him in a blind place. Cracks appear. And the silence—
a silence that starts so deep
under the rock

he can hear it ringing. Man is a slave and a sombre being.
Who does not know enough to lick the salt
off the low bushes at dawn.

TV is loud, yet we do not awake.

V.

TV wastes nothing, like a wife.

While Hektor was out making war, his wife heated water on the fire
for a bath when he returned wearied of killing.
Later that night

they brought news of his death. She puts away the water
and uses the fire to burn all his clothes.
Since they will be no benefit to you,

nor will you wear them, she says. Looking out over the parapet
to the arc-lit battlefield where men
with string

were measuring the distance from Hektor's darkening nipple
to the camera's eye.
She saw men on their knees.

VI.

From the helicopter Death Valley looks like an entrail.
Vast coiling cracks of gold and grey lunge endlessly across it—
Run Hektor!

rasps the director from the walkie-talkie
as the helicopter goes squalling past Hektor's head
and the downdraft

knocks him flat. Plunged into the depths of encircling walls
an animal will lose its tuning knob.
Hektor was

for Troy a source of food, a cause for exultation in prayer,
a likeness of God,
a human glory.

He had constructed throughout Troy a system of gutters,
which ran along both sides of every street,
squared with stone

in alternating blocks of polished and unpolished agate.
Waters ran quietly out of Troy.
Now Hektor worries

that stains on the back of his clothing will be visible
from the helicopter as he turns
to run.

TV is made of light, like shame.

VII.

As the bottom of a sea, which it once was, Death Valley is perpetually
in motion.
A thin
silver
pressure rakes the dunes from north to west forming parallel grooves
miles
wide
that vanish in half an hour and vanish again, tarrying and driving on,
marking,
blanking.
As the kings of Troy comb out their hair before battle
into
patterns
no one can remember after, Hektor is running
the
length
of a gravel groove heading straight for Troy.

He
can
just see his wife on the parapet waving a piece of clothing.
He
waves
too. He will never reach her. Under his feet the sand is shifting,
its
slight
incomprehensible ball bearings carrying him ever more west
and
south
toward the unclocked clarity of his last and inland sea.

TV is a condition of weightless balance, like a game.
But TV is not a game.

VIII.

TV comes out of the dark, like Hektor's prayer verbs.

To blue.
To tear from the midpoint.
To lay bare crystals.
To lay bare a sky.
To ash.
To put silence over it.
To not desist.
To inmost.
To mount smoke (of a soul).

IX.

TV has a glare to it, like Hektor's prayer.

YOU PART. ENDANGERED WE.
HANG.
PERSONS OF ASH.

ASHED.

X.

Late each night in his motel room Hektor puts on a headset
to shut out the noise of the keno lounge next door
and sits down to write a postcard to his wife.

VERY COLD IN THE DESERT WE SHOOT FROM DAWN TO DUSK
MILITARY JETS CAVORTING OVERHEAD THE DIRECTOR RED
WITH RAGE NO TIME FOR LUNCH *THE LIGHT IS GOING!* YOU
WOULD LIKE MY COSTUME IT IS SILK THANK YOU FOR THE
YEARS THEY TASTE LIKE HOME
P

Then he takes out a big red notebook from the desk drawer
and puts on a sweater and sits again. Staring hard.
DIARY FOR MYSELF ALONE says the cover.

Today Hektor fought like a boulder going downhill.
Torn from the rockface it bounds and flies, treetops
roar past underneath,
nothing can stop it—
hits the plain!
There he was stabbing away at a wall of skirmishers.
Like a flashing snowpeak he moved,
like a wave exploding foam, like a giant breaker
boiling toward the beach—

By now morning fires are being kindled throughout the motel.
Dawn pots are banging.
Hektor works on,

while behind him, the long blades of his spears and harpoons
stand propped on the wall
beside the TV—

there he was
testing the enemy line at every point
to see where it would give!
The deaf day moved toward ox-time.
Truth
rolled away from him
under the cannon-bones of the night.

TV uses for "grave" the word "sign," like Homer.

XI.

TV is presocial, like Man.

On the last day of the Death Valley shoot
driving through huge slow brown streaks of mountain
towards the light-hole,

Hektor feels his pits go dry.

Clouds drop their lines down the faces of the rock
as if marking out a hunting ground.
Hektor, whose heart

walked ahead of him always,

ran ahead like a drunk creature
to lick salt particles off the low bushes
as if they were butter or silver honey,

whose heart Homer compared to a lion

turning in a net of dogs and men and
whichever way the lion lunges the men and dogs give way
yet the net keeps contracting—

Hektor trembles.

The human way includes two kinds of knowledge.
Fire and Night. Hektor has been to the Fire
in conditions of experimental purity.

It is 6:53 A.M. when his Night unhoods itself.

Hektor sees that he is lying at the centre of a vast metal disc.
A dawn clot of moon dangles oddly above
and this realization comes coldly through him:

the disc is tilting.

Very slowly the disc attains an angle of thirty degrees.
Dark blue signal is flowing steadily
from the centre to the edge

as Hektor starts to slide.

It takes but an instant to realize you are mortal.
Troy reared up on its hind legs
and a darkness of life flowed through the town

from purple cup to purple cup.

Toes to the line please, says the assistant camera man,
slapping two pieces of yellow tape
on the surface of the disc

just in front of Hektor's feet.

Dashing back to the camera he raises his slate.
Places everyone, calls the director as a thousand wasps
come stinging out of the arc lamp

and the camera is pouring its black butter,

its bitter honey,
straight into Hektor's eye.
Hektor steps to the line.

War has always interested me, he begins.

TV Men: Artaud

Artaud is mad.
He stayed close to the madness. Watching it breathe or not breathe.
There is a close-up of me driven to despair.

His face is mad.
It was something of fire on which his soul wrote. All this mental glass.
Me beating my head against a wall.

His body is mad.
Some days he felt uterine. Mind screwed into him by a thrust of sky.
I run among the ruins.

His mind is mad.
There was (he decided) no mind. The body (hell) just as you see it.
Go throw myself from the tower, gesticulating, falling.

His hospital is mad.
He noted in electric shock a splash state. What holes, and made of what?
Falling to the beach.

His Mexico is mad.
There was not a shadow he did not count. No opium, no heads on the days.
You see my body crumpled on the sand.

His God is mad.
He felt God pulling him out through his own cunt. Claque. Claque-dents.
It moves convulsively a few times.

His double is mad.
The drawback of being mad was that he could not both be so and say so.
Beautiful jerks.

His word is mad.
He had to become an enigma to himself. To prevent his own theft of him.
You see my battered face.

His excrement is mad.
He envied bones their purity. Hated to die *rectified* (as he said) by pain.
Then I fall back.

His spring snow is mad.
They found him at dawn. Seated at the foot of his bed. Holding his shoe.
And shy away.

TV Men: Sokrates

Before the robin's red surmise we were at the prison gates
on Sokrates' death day.

Like Silenos discovered asleep in his cave
by two boys

who fetter his enemy legs before he awakes
lest he

once more deceive them in their hope of a song, Sokrates
opens his—

eyes stacked with the motions of roses in that other dawn
and a torn coolness—

reluctantly. It is so early,
why are you here?

he says. I like the word *krisis* which Sokrates taught me.
It means Decision.

Ruling (of a court). Middle (of the spinal column).
Our first shot

is Sokrates tapping the sleep spine—out pours his own dream:
a woman

in white who spoke to him in his sleep. *Krisis* means
the crack that runs

between Sokrates sitting on the edge of his bunk telling us Death Is
No Misfortune

and his soul making little twitchy moves against the flesh,
which show up

on the film as bright dots or phosphorescence before
storms.

We pan away along the length of the prison corridor as it goes curving
very gradually

past the cells of the other prisoners which are dug into the ground
like intervals

of sanity and burn with a bluish glow. Back in his cell Sokrates is calm.
His little song,

in a voice wavering, collapsing, sucked under here and there
by secret

heat like someone going too fast so we speeded up the film
and speed

made no difference—he was up there in a clear place, as a player
may rest

against the laws of the game. But *TV Is Not A Game* was the name of his song.
He sang it

through to the end. Pale dawn was filling the lap of the room.
We filmed

his feet, legs, knees, upper legs and when the camera reached his heart
we had

almost 5 minutes of film left and I said to him, Stay! and he said,
Why?

and he was gone. Those who make pledges in their sleep shall in their
sleep
keep them.

On our way out the guard mentioned some cigarettes Sokrates had
asked him to get,

never paid for. He suggested we settle the bill.
Which we did.

TV Men: The Sleeper

The sleeper, real and dear, is carved on the dark.
Minerals of sleep are travelling into him.
Travelling out of him.
Signal leaps in his wrist.
Caught to me, caught to my nerve.

Night kneels over the sleeper.
Where did his journey begin, where will
it burn through to?
And what does he swim for now.
Swim, sleeper, swim.

Your peace as an evangelist to me.
Your transformations unknown.
I study your sleeping form
at the bottom of the pool
like a house I could return to,

like a head to be cradled in the arms.
Unless you are asleep I cannot make my way
across the night
and through my isolation.
Your small hands lap at the wave.

And contradict everything here, your passion
a whole darkness swung against the kind of sleep we
know,
the stumbled-into sleep of lanterns clipped on for a tour of the mine.
You dove once

into your privatest presentiment
and stayed, face down in your black overcoat.
To my wonder.
Endlessness runs in you like leaves on the tree of night.
To live here one must forget much.

TV Men: Sappho

avec ma main brûlée j'écris sur la nature du feu

I.

No one knows what the laws are. That there are laws
we know, by the daily burnings if nothing else.
On the second

day of shooting in the Place de la Concorde
I notice the leaves in the Jardin have changed
overnight,

but mention this to no one
for fear of continuity problems.
I had already invalidated 16 (otherwise good)

takes this morning by changing an earring.
You cannot erase.
Is this a law?

No, a talent. To step obliquely
where stones are sharp.
Vice is also sharp.

There are laws against vice.
But the shock stays with you.

II.

la vie est brève
un peu d'amour
un peu de rêve
ainsi bonjour

The Talent has a talent
for the obvious.
See this rope?

Tie one end to me
and the other to Death:
overlit on all fours I shall

circle Him
at a consistent focal length.
Not too close not too far—

("Home," whispers the cameraman
as the gravestones in the background
spill slowly

out of the frame.)
Earth will be warmer than we thought,
after all this circling.

THE FALL OF ROME: A TRAVELLER'S GUIDE

I.
By this time tomorrow I will be a man of Rome.

II.
I
am

going

to
visit
Anna Xenia.

III.
Long cold fingers
dipped in blue roses

pry open the red world.

A motionless aeroplane
goes shrieking over
the oceans of Europe.

IV.
The captain has turned on the FASTEN SEATBELT sign.

V.
Anna Xenia will be waking now.

VI.
We fall helplessly into Rome.

VII.
Who I am doesn't matter.
As you see me

fighting to survive,

fighting to be esteemed and honoured
(so that my past vanishes),
you will dismiss me as nothing terrific.

Fair enough
but there is one thing about me:
I can take you to Anna Xenia.

VIII.
She is a citizen of the ancient republic.
historian of its wars

and ravishing

in
her
armour.

IX.
Now although I hate to travel
I go a lot of places

and have noted

certain recurrent phenomena.
A journey, for example,
begins with a voice

calling your name out
behind you.
This seems a convenient arrangement.

How else would you know it's time to go?
On the other hand,
who is it?

And what do they want?
So too a friendship
begins before the first meeting,

an empire
before the first conquest.
Anna Xenia has studied at Oxford.

Maybe
she can explain
some of this to me.

X.
First meeting.
Pacing the sidewalk in front of my hotel

in a sweat, will she look different? do I look

different? what if I don't recognize—perhaps
she is here already!—I wheel:
there.

She is. Smiling hard.
Holding five gigantic red flowers
upside down (Roman custom?) at which

I clutch,
all language vanished from my mind.
We knock each other over

in a violent embrace
and hurtle off
to find Rome.

XI.
What is the holiness of the citizen?
It is to open

a day

to a stranger,
who has no day
of his own.

XII.
There is a wonderful lot of talk in Rome.
I walk about in it

moving zigzag,

parting it like a comb.
hearing it coil
together

behind me.
Entrata.
Uscita.

XIII.
A stranger makes no fissure.

XIV.
Second meeting.
When I think I have walked enough

I go to Anna Xenia's.

She is as beautiful as an island.
She looms on tiny hooves
and makes Nescafé.

There is a wonderful lot of talk in Anna Xenia.
She cocks her head like Cicero
and pretends

I am someone talking back.
Good afternoon.
I'm well thanks how are you?

XV.
From deep within
my traveller's clothes

I watch these conversations take place.

Italian is a beautiful language,
also very difficult.
So long.

XVI.
Then I return to my hotel.
Take off the big coat.

Hang up

the enormous trousers.
Sit down to wait
for the nightmare.

XVII.
As the master of the day is Anna Xenia,
the master

of the night

is dread.
I position myself.
It fills up the room.

XVIII.
It seeps beneath doors,
beneath sleep,

it fills up the bed,

the corridor,
it rises to cover Entrata
and Uscita,

no way out,
no way in,
a stranger

sleeps
in a solution of dread.
Romans hate a stranger.

XIX.
Why have you
come here?

You

have
broken in,
why?

XX.
I think I will call my nightmare The Fall Of Rome.

XXI.
Alaric invaded Rome in 410 AD.
The nightmare

was waiting for him.

He stayed three days.
Entrata.
Uscita.

XXII.
What was the holiness
of Alaric?

It was to run

and keep
running.
Out the dawn side.

XXIII.
A stranger is someone who runs by night
down streets where Alaric ran,

falling in a nightmare of God.

Excuse me please tell me, which way to the exit? Entrata.
Entrata.
Entrata.

Sores breaking out.
What is the holiness of the stranger?
He has none.

XXIV.
A stranger is poor, voracious and turbulent.
He comes

from nowhere in particular

and pushes prices up.
His method of knowing something
is to eat it.

XXV.
Yes, Romans hate a stranger.
Swaying miraculously on their stilts

Romans stand for a state of civilization.

With the names of the cities
and rivers
and principal provinces

clearly marked.
With the seats of disease
identified.

With the holy days
lit in a row.
No

grinning.
No
nakedness.

XXVI.
How do Romans know
who is the stranger?

Pronto.

Evil picks him out.
Anna Xenia explained this to me.
"Every stranger is a villain in the true sense."

XXVII.
You think I am talking about jet lag,
a touch of insomnia,

a little traveller's ennui.

No.
I hate to bother you,
but I am talking about evil.

It blooms.
It eats.
It grins.

It has 28 eyes.
You can see it racing down the centuries of all the strangers
who have come here—

since Aeneas,
for all I know.
wings outspread.

A stranger is evil.
The sores may be so thick-matted
you can hardly see

his ears and tail,
but no Roman
is fooled by that.

If he weren't evil he wouldn't be
a stranger,
would he?

XXVIII.
Now,

I have a tendency to dread.
I have to watch it.

XXIX.
I grin.
I eat.

Thousand of cuts morning and night,

practising fierce techniques of horrible war! useless.
Dread masters me.
I do not master dread.

XXX.
A stranger is master of nothing.

Who in a nightmare
can help himself?

XXXI.
On the other hand,
it gives me a pretext

for travel (travel

justifies dread:
other places really are
terrible).

XXXII.
And besides, in this case
there is no mistake.

Romans do hate (as I say)

a stranger. And
their reasoning
is empirically

sound.
What is the holiness of empire?
It is to know collapse.

Everything can collapse.
Houses, bodies
and enemies

collapse
when their rhythm becomes
deranged.

XXXIII.
Rome collapsed when Alaric ran out the dawn side.

XXXIV.
A stranger is someone who comes on the wrong day.

XXXV.
Forgets to telephone.

XXXVI.
And interrupts the Roman at his work.

XXXVII.
You are asking for trouble
if you surprise a Roman

on a day

when he thinks he is free
of public
performance.

XXXVIII.
He will come to the door of his cage
as cold and furious

as that beast whose tawny skull

he loves to smash
on other days of the week
in the name of the *Pax Romana*.

XXXIX.
A stranger is someone who stands in the doorway,
drenched in confusion,

and permits the dog to escape.

Anna Xenia chases the dog
down five flights.
She comes back

to find me still in the doorway.
It is a difficult moment.
Third meeting.

XL.
Excuse me, may I come in, nonetheless?
Shall I sit down, all the same?

A stranger is someone desperate for conversation.

Then why is it I never have anything to say?
We perch in our armour
at the kitchen table.

Lunch has been cleared away
and she has got her smile up
as far as the mouth.

Please speak more slowly.
It is my first visit
to Rome.

XLI.
Faced with a villain
a Roman knows what to do.

Rant.

Papal history. The
persecution of Tasso.
The pomposity

of Seneca.
The insincerity of the Communist Party Secretary of Rome
(whose wife collects topaz).

The landlady.
The doorlocks.
The plumbing—

XLII.
it is noble.

Like Cicero adressing the Senate,
Anna Xenia grows as she talks—

XLIII.
she pauses mid-tide ("Shall I

make us some Nescafé?") just as
the waterpipes gasp and go dry.

XLIV.
A stranger is someone
who sits

very still at the kitchen table,

looks down at his knuckles,
thinks some day we will laugh about this,
doesn't believe it.

XLV.
"Uccidi! flagella! brucia!"
I beg you.

"This Roman water!"

What is the problem?
"Shuts itself off whenever it likes!"
What is the reason?

"There is no reason!"
Shall we notify someone?
"There is no one to notify!"

What can we do?
"There is nothing we can do!"
I have brought with me to Rome

(as you advised)
Helpful Phrases For Travellers
in the pocket Italian

edition.
Helpful phrases come to mind.
Please show me to the lifeboat.

XLVI.
A stranger is someone
who knows little of plumbing.

If water stops

he goes to another city,
washes his face
in acqua minerale,

or begins a novena.
And helpful phrases
lie close at hand.

I see we have a breakdown.
May I speak to the manager?
Where does one get the train for Milan?

XLVII.
But in a Roman life
are only impossibilities.

Che posso farci?

Nothing you can do.
It is simply a bad, implacable Roman fact
like the way they drive.

XLVIII.
Nevertheless, I feel I should say something.

XLIX.
I lunge for words.
She knocks them away.

At one point (how stupid

can a stranger be?)
I even ask her about God!
This is terrible. This is

broad daylight and the nightmare
is filling up the room.
Senza uscita.

L.
You don't remember me at all, do you?

LI.
A stranger is someone who walks in
and for an instant

I don't know it is you—

an instant
almost as troubling as death,
or so

some believe,
for example
Proust:

". . . c'est admettre que ce qui était ici,
l'être qu'on se rappelle n'est plus,
et que ce qui y est,

c'est un être qu'on on ne connaissait pas;
c'est avoir à penser un mystère
presque aussi troublant

que celui de la mort dont il est,
du reste,
comme la préface et l'annonciateur."

Now Proust
spent no time in Rome.
And he has a complex way

of understanding what a stranger is
(he gets it inside out)
which would not stand

Roman scrutiny.
Nonetheless,
his piercing eyes

open wide
on what the real trouble is.
It is that voice behind you.

LII.
For, if you think about it,
all first hatred of strangers

contains this idea of death,

of your death which will one day walk up to you
in just such a fashion.
Buon giorno, death will say.

LIII.
What is the holiness of conversation?

It is
to master death.

LIV.
You think I am being melodramatic.
One awful conversation about waterpipes.

isn't the end of a friendship.

Well, a stranger is someone
who takes dread a little too seriously.
Out

on the street again at sunset,
sores open,
moving blindly.

There is a loneliness that fills the plain.
Total.
Lunar.

Who in a nightmare can help himself?
Good morning.
Excuse me.

Good night.
Yes this is my (our) first trip to Rome.
I am (we are) having a topnotch time.

May I introduce you to my (our) wife (husband,
son, daughter, mother, father, masculine friend,
feminine friend)?

You are welcome.
You are very welcome.
It is two

in the morning.
I would like to speak to the chief of police.
There is a black planet speeding towards us.

LV.
Fifth meeting.
When she smiles like that

she is as beautiful as all my secrets.

Anna Xenia has decided
we must visit Orvieto.
A thing like this can save a stranger's life.

LVI.
For Anna Xenia,
as for most Romans,

driving is war.

Perhaps, on the way to Orvieto,
she will explain to me
why this is so?

Yes (slams horn) naturalmente!
Her explanation is lengthy.
Well exampled (horn).

Solidly convincing.
At the end she pauses.
Short silence.

Suddenly
a whoop of laughter
and she slaps the steering wheel.

"You're right,
there's no reason at all!"
It delights her all the way to Orvieto.

LVII.
Now,
Orvieto.

The city is of Etruscan origin,

once a papal stronghold.
On top
arises

a pedestal of volcanic rock.
On top of the rock is a word.
In the years from 1290 to 1600,

there were 33 architects,
152 sculptors,
68 painters

and 90 mosaicists
at work shaping the word
into a cathedral.

They covered the outside
with jewels and stones and gold.
They filled the inside

with 17 perfect horizontal stripes,
in alternating courses of black and white stone,
60 metres long.

They inflected the word
into one clear command.
Think of it.

Think what it means
to be a stranger
and to walk into the word "Live!"

LVIII.
For the first time since I came to Rome
I am thinking beyond death.

I laugh.

She looks.
She laughs.
It is sunset

and we are driving home.
Masters
of entrata and uscita.

LIX.
What is the holiness of mastery?

Let us help ourselves
to a theory of the martial arts.

LX.
It is to cut your opponent
just at the moment he cuts you.

This is the ultimate timing.

It is lack of anger.
It means to treat your enemy
as an honoured guest.

LXI.
Besides the cathedral,
at Orvieto there is

a second tourist attraction.

It is a well.
The Pozzo di San Patrizio
was built by Pope Clement VII

to supply the town with water
in case of a siege.
It is over 62 metres deep.

There are 248 comfortable steps
from the top to the bottom of the well: 248 spiral back up.
They are not the same steps.

LXII.
Designed concentrically
the two staircases fit

one within the other

like a jackknife blade
within a jackknife,
so that two people

one coming up,
the other going down,
can never meet.

LXIII.
Meanwhile I know you will be pleased
if I leave with you

to chew over in your own time,

a small question of interpretation
which arose out of my visit to Orvieto.
The cathedral contains a chapel,

now known as the Signorelli Chapel,
decorated in 1499 with monumental frescoes,
painted pilasters, panels of grotesques

and false windows
by the famed Luca Signorelli
for a fee of 180 ducats paid *pro rata*.

Around the lower walls of the chapel
Signorelli has added
a series of grisaille medallions

illustrating scenes from Dante's *Comedia*.
They are monochrome,
eerie in appearance

and iconologically
controversial.
For example,

one medallion depicts the scene from *Purgatorio* III
where Dante is accosted by a mob of souls.
They are demanding an answer.

E urgente.
Permesso?
They point.

Dante's text makes clear
that it is Dante's shadow
which has mastered the attention of the whimpering shades,

for throughout the *Purgatorio* (you well know)
only Dante,
as a living man,

casts a shadow.
Dante makes no mistake
about what the laws of optics require here.

Shadow is a matter of interception of light.
The dead intercept nothing. Capisco.
Much less clear

is Signorelli's rendering of the scene.
He had given everyone a shadow.
Why?

The standard guidebook explanation
fails to nourish me:
". . . Signorelli has assigned shadows

to all his figures,
unable to suppress
his naturalistic training

even at the expense of poetic veracity."
Non capisco.
I point.

LXIV.
There are three ways to master death.
Here is the third one (the one

Anna Xenia told me

on the way home from Orvieto).
Signorelli is painting late in his studio
when they carry in his son,

killed in a riot.
He sits up all night with the body,
making sketch after sketch

and throwing them into a pile.
From that time
all his angels

have the one
same
face.

LXV.
Sixth meeting.
Three years ago today

Anna Xenia's son died

on a night of heavy rain and bad traffic.
He was broken but lucid.
"What time is it?"

he kept asking.
It is two in the morning.
"No!

Impossible!
Look at the light pouring there!"
He points.

LXVI.
Her marble tears run down her marble face.
A stranger is someone who has no handkerchief.

Who has no words to say.

Whose shadow mind is burning
as he sits watching her hands
and thinks how rare!

to see a Roman
talk
with no gestures at all.

LXVII.
There are divers things you can learn
from a guidebook.

The Hachette Guide To France, for example,

provides four pages of maps showing
distribution of roof styles,
while Osamu Dazai's

Travels Of A Purple Tramp
mainly relates the regrets
of this sad and stumbling person,

and how much he drank,
on the way to visit his hometown of Tsugaru.
From Marco Polo you find out

exactly how to get to China.
From Herodotos,
a theory of why

Egyptian women urinate standing up
(because the men do it sitting down).
A traveller can warn you

of climate
or prices
or other people's etiquette

and make himself useful
in fond and sharpening ways.
But no.

LXVIII.
Instead,
I pour over you

this bath of dread.

Why is a nightmare
drawing a circle
around us?

LXIX.
Last meeting.
Anna Xenia is at my hotel very early,

dressed in red.

It is important to strike a positive note,
towards the end.
I (we) have had a topnotch time.

Italian has proven a beautiful language,
also very difficult.
On this,

my first visit to Rome,
I have mastered a few words
(entrata, uscita)

and suppressed others
(villano, morte).
You have been most kind,

in speaking slowly
and inviting me in for Nescafé.
Although tongue-tied myself,

your conversation has led me to uncover
certain false answers
to life's basic questions

(That stranger was myself! etc.)
Once or twice we spoke our hearts:
"cet immense désir de connaître la vie"

as Proust so simply calls it.
Please summon a porter.
It is time to go.

LXX.
We kiss in slow motion.
She turns and heads off

in her small red soldier's coat.

Off, and stepping cleanly
toward the first day of school.
Off and down the ramp,

almost deaf in the glare of the white sand ahead,
the tiny gladiator,
stuffing her shadow into her mouth as she goes.

Until
we meet again.
So long.

BOOK OF ISAIAH

I.

Isaiah awoke angry.

Lapping at Isaiah's ears black birdsong no it was anger.

God had filled Isaiah's ears with stingers.

Once God and Isaiah were friends.

God and Isaiah used to converse nightly, Isaiah would rush into the garden.

They conversed under the Branch, night streamed down.

From the sole of the foot to the head God would make Isaiah ring.

Isaiah had loved God and now his love was turned to pain.

Isaiah wanted a name for the pain, he called it sin.

Now Isaiah was a man who believed he was a nation.

Isaiah called the nation Judah and the sin Judah's condition.

Inside Isaiah God saw the worldsheet burning.

Isaiah and God saw things differently, I can only tell you their actions.

Isaiah addressed the nation.

Man's brittleness! cried Isaiah.

The nation stirred in its husk and slept again.

Two slabs of bloody meat lay folded on its eyes like wings.

Like a hard glossy painting the nation slept.

Who can invent a new fear?

Yet I have invented sin, thought Isaiah, running his hand over the knobs.

And then, because of a great attraction between them—

which Isaiah fought (for and against) for the rest of his life—

God shattered Isaiah's indifference.

God washed Isaiah's hair in fire.

God took the stay.

From beneath its meat wings the nation listened.

You, said Isaiah.

No answer.

I cannot hear you, Isaiah spoke again under the Branch.

Light bleached open the night camera.

God arrived.

God smashed Isaiah like glass through every socket of his nation.

Liar! said God.

Isaiah put his hands on his coat, he put his hand on his face.

Isaiah is a small man, said Isaiah, but no liar.

God paused.

And so that was their contract.

Brittle on both sides, no lying.

Isaiah's wife came to the doorway, the doorposts had moved.

What's that sound? said Isaiah's wife.

The fear of the Lord, said Isaiah.

He grinned in the dark, she went back inside.

Book Of Isaiah

II.

There is a kind of pressure in humans to take whatever is most
beloved by them
and smash it.

Religion calls the pressure *piety* and the smashed thing *a sacrifice to
God.*

Prophets question these names.

What is an idol?

An idol is a useless sacrifice, said Isaiah.

But how do you know which ones are useless? asked the nation in its
genius.

Isaiah pondered the various ways he could answer this.

Immense chunks of natural reality fell out of a blue sky
and showers of light upon his mind.

Isaiah chose the way of metaphor.

Our life is a *camera obscura,* said Isaiah, do you know what that is?

Never heard of it, said the nation.

Imagine yourself in a darkened room, Isaiah instructed.

Okay, said the nation.

The doors are closed, there is a pinhole in the back wall.

A pinhole, the nation repeated.

Light shoots through the pinhole and strikes the opposite wall.

The nation was watching Isaiah, bored and fascinated at once.

You can hold up anything you like in front of that pinhole, said Isaiah,
and worship it on the opposite wall.

Why worship an image? asked the nation.

Exactly, said Isaiah.

The nation chewed on that for a moment.

Then its genius spoke up.

So what about Isaiah's pinhole?

Ah, said Isaiah.

A memory fell through him as clear heat falls on herbs.

Isaiah remembered the old days, conversing with God under the Branch

and like an old butler waking in an abandoned house the day the revolution began,

Isaiah bent his head.

A burden was upon Isaiah.

Isaiah opened his mouth.

A sigh came from Isaiah's mouth, the sigh grew into a howl.

The howl ran along the brooks to the mouth of the brooks

and tore the nets of the fishers who cast angle into the brooks

and confounded the workers in fine flax who weave networks

and broke their purpose.

The howl rolled like a rolling thing past slain men and harvests and spoils

and stopped in a ditch between two walls.

Then Isaiah unclamped his mouth from the howl.

Isaiah let his mouth go from the teat.

Isaiah turned, Isaiah walked away.

Isaiah walked for three years naked and barefoot with buttocks uncovered
to the shame of the nation.

All night you could see the Branch roaming against the sky like a soul.

Book Of Isaiah

III.

Isaiah walked for three years in the valley of vision.

In his jacket of glass he crossed deserts and black winter mornings.

The icy sun lowered its eyelids against the glare of him.

God stayed back.

Now Isaiah had a hole in the place where his howl had broken off.

All the while Isaiah walked, Isaiah's heart was pouring out the hole.

One day Isaiah stopped.

Isaiah put his hand on the amputated place.

Isaiah's heart is small but in a way sacred, said Isaiah, I will save it.

Isaiah plugged the hole with millet and dung.

God watched Isaiah's saving action.

God was shaking like an olive tree.

Now or never, whispered God.

God reached down and drew a line on the floor of the desert in front of Isaiah's feet.

Silence began.

Silence roared down the canals of Isaiah's ears into his brain.

Isaiah was listening to the silence.

Deep under it was another sound Isaiah could hear miles down.

A sort of ringing.

Wake up Isaiah! said God from behind Isaiah's back.

Isaiah jumped and spun around.

Wake up and praise God! said God smiling palely.

Isaiah spat.

God thought fast.

The nation is burning! God cried pointing across the desert.

Isaiah looked.

All the windows of the world stood open and blowing.

In each window Isaiah saw a motion like flames.

Behind the flames he saw a steel fence lock down.

Caught between the flames and the fence was a deer.

Isaiah saw the deer of the nation burning all along its back.

In its amazement the deer turned and turned and turned

until its own shadow lay tangled around its feet like melted wings.

Isaiah reached out both his hands, they flared in the dawn.

Poor flesh! said Isaiah.

Your nation needs you Isaiah, said God.

Flesh breaks, Isaiah answered. Everyone's will break. There is nothing we can do.

I tell you Isaiah you can save the nation.

The wind was rising, God was shouting.

You can strip it down, start over at the wires, use lions! use thunder! *use what you see—*

Isaiah was watching sweat and tears run down God's face.

Okay, said Isaiah, so I save the nation. What do *you* do?

God exhaled roughly.

I save the fire, said God.

Thus their contract continued.

Book Of Isaiah

IV.

When Isaiah came back in from the desert centuries had passed.

There was nothing left of Isaiah but a big forehead.

The forehead went rolling around the nation and spoke to people who leapt to their feet
and fled.

If the nation had taken Isaiah to court he could have proven his righteousness.

But they met in secret and voted to cut him off.

Shepherds! Chosen ones! Skinny dogs! Blood of a dog! Watchmen all! said Isaiah.

Isaiah withdrew to the Branch.

It was a blue winter evening, the cold bit like a wire.

Isaiah laid his forehead on the ground.

God arrived.

Why do the righteous suffer? said Isaiah.

Bellings of cold washed down the Branch.

Notice whenever God addresses Isaiah in a feminine singular verb something dazzling is
about to happen.

Isaiah what do you know about women? asked God.

Down Isaiah's nostrils bounced woman words:

Blush. Stink. Wife. Fig. Sorceress—

God nodded.

Isaiah go home and get some sleep, said God.

Isaiah went home, slept, woke again.

Isaiah felt sensation below the neck, it was a silk and bitter sensation.

Isaiah looked down.

It was milk forcing the nipples open.

Isaiah was more than whole.

I am not with you I am *in* you, said the muffled white voice of God.

Isaiah sank to a kneeling position.

New pain! said Isaiah.

New contract! said God.

Isaiah lifted his arms, milk poured out his breasts.

Isaiah watched the milk pour like strings.

It poured up the Branch and across history and down into people's lives and time.

The milk made Isaiah forget about righteousness.

As he fed the milk to small birds and animals Isaiah thought only about their little lips.

God meanwhile continued to think about male and female.

After all there are two words for righteousness, Isaiah could not be expected to untie this
hard knot himself.

First the masculine word TSDQ, a bolt of justice that splits the oak in two.

Then in the empty muscle of the wood, mushrooms and maggots and monkeys set up a
livelihood:

here is (the feminine word) TSDQH.

God grave the two words on Isaiah's palms.

God left it at that.

And although it is true Isaiah's prophecies continued to feature *eunuch cylinders* and
clickfoot woman shame.

And although it is true Isaiah himself knew several wives and begot a bastard son.

Still some nights through his dreams slipped a river of milk.

A river of silver, a river of pity.

He slept, the asters in the garden unloaded their red thunder into the dark.

THE GENDER OF SOUND

It is in large part according to the sounds people make that we judge them sane or insane, male or female, good, evil, trustworthy, depressive, marriageable, moribund, likely or unlikely to make war on us, little better than animals, inspired by God. These judgments happen fast and can be brutal. Aristotle tells us that the highpitched voice of the female is one evidence of her evil disposition, for creatures who are brave or just (like lions, bulls, roosters and the human male) have large deep voices.[1] If you hear a man talking in a gentle or highpitched voice you know he is a *kinaidos* ("catamite").[2] The poet Aristophanes puts a comic turn on this cliché in his *Ekklesiazousai*: as the women of Athens are about to infiltrate the Athenian assembly and take over political process, the feminist leader Praxagora reassures her fellow female activists that they have precisely the right kind of voices for this task. Because, as she says, "You know that among the young men the ones who turn out to be terrific talkers are the ones who get fucked a lot."[3]

This joke depends on a collapsing together of two different aspects of sound production, quality of voice and use of voice. We will find the ancients continually at pains to associate these two aspects under a general rubric of gender. High vocal pitch goes together with talkativeness to characterize a person who is deviant from or deficient in the masculine ideal of self-control. Women, catamites, eunuchs and androgynes fall into this category. Their sounds are bad to hear and make men uncomfortable. Just how uncomfortable may be measured by the lengths to which Aristotle is willing to go in accounting for the gender of sound physiognomically; he ends up ascribing the lower pitch of the male voice to the tension placed on a man's vocal chords by his testicles functioning as loom weights.[4] In Hellenistic and Roman times doctors recommended vocal exercises to cure all sorts of physical and psychological ailments in men, on the theory that the practice of declamation would relieve congestion in the head and correct the damage that men habitually do to themselves in daily life by using the voice for highpitched sounds, loud shouting or aimless conversation. Here again we note a confusion of vocal quality and vocal use. This therapy was not on the whole recommended to women or eunuchs or androgynes, who were believed to have the wrong kind of flesh and the wrong alignment of pores for the production of low vocal pitches, no matter how hard they exercised. But for the masculine physique vocal practice was thought an effective way to restore body and mind by pulling the voice back down to appropriately manly pitches.[5] I have a friend who is a radio journalist and he assures me that these suppositions about voice quality are still with us. He is a man and he is gay. He spent the first several years of his career in radio fending off the attempts of producers to deepen, darken and depress his voice, which they described as "having too much smile in it." Very few women in public life do not worry that their voices are too high or too light or too shrill to command respect. Margaret Thatcher trained for years with a vocal coach to make her voice sound more like those of the other Honourable Members and still earned the nickname *Attila The Hen*.[6] This hen analogy goes back to the publicity surrounding Nancy Astor, first female member of the British House Of Commons in 1919, who was described by her colleague Sir Henry Channon as "a queer combination of warmheartedness, originality and rudeness . . . she rushes about like a decapitated hen . . . intriguing and enjoying the smell of blood . . . the mad witch."[7] Madness and witchery as well as bestiality are conditions commonly associated with the use of the female voice in public, in ancient as well as modern contexts. Consider how many female celebrities of classical mythology, literature and cult make themselves objectionable by the way they use their voice. For example there is the heartchilling groan of the Gorgon, whose name is derived from a Sanskrit word **garg* meaning "a guttural animal howl that issues as a great wind from the back of the throat through a hugely distended mouth."[8] There are the Furies whose highpitched and horrendous voices are compared by Aiskhylos to howling dogs or sounds of people being tortured in hell (*Eumenides*).[9] There is the deadly voice of the Sirens and the dangerous ventriloquism of Helen (*Odyssey*)[10] and the incredible babbling of Kassandra (Aiskhylos, *Agamemnon*)[11] and the fearsome hullabaloo of Artemis as she charges through the woods (*Homeric Hymn to Aphrodite*).[12] There is the seductive discourse of

Aphrodite which is so concrete an aspect of her power that she can wear it on her belt as a physical object or lend it to other women (*Iliad*).[13] There is the old woman of Eleusinian legend Iambe who shrieks obscenities and throws her skirt up over her head to expose her genitalia.[14] There is the haunting garrulity of the nymph Echo (daughter of Iambe in Athenian legend) who is described by Sophokles as "the girl with no door on her mouth" (*Philoktetes*).[15]

Putting a door on the female mouth has been an important project of patriarchal culture from antiquity to the present day. Its chief tactic is an ideological association of female sound with monstrosity, disorder and death. Consider this description by one of her biographers of the sound of Gertrude Stein:

> Gertrude was hearty. She used to roar with laughter, out loud. She had a laugh like a beefsteak. She loved beef.[16]

These sentences, with their artful confusion of factual and metaphorical levels, carry with them as it seems to me a whiff of pure fear. It is a fear that projects Gertrude Stein across the boundary of woman and human and animal kind into monstrosity. The simile "she had a laugh like a beefsteak" which identifies Gertrude Stein with cattle is followed at once by the statement "she loved beef" indicating that Gertrude Stein ate cattle. Creatures who eat their own kind are regularly called cannibals and regarded as abnormal. Gertrude Stein's other abnormal attributes, notably her large physical size and lesbianism, were emphasized persistently by critics, biographers and journalists who did not know what to make of her prose. The marginalization of her personality was a way to deflect her writing from literary centrality. If she is fat, funny-looking and sexually deviant she must be a marginal talent, is the assumption.

One of the literary patriarchs who feared Gertrude Stein most was Ernest Hemingway. And it is interesting to hear him tell the story of how he came to end his friendship with Gertrude Stein because he could not tolerate the sound of her voice. The story takes place in Paris. Hemingway tells it from the point of view of a disenchanted expatriate just realizing that he cannot after all make a life for himself amid the alien culture where he is stranded. One spring day in 1924

Hemingway comes to call on Gertrude Stein and is admitted by the maid:

> The maidservant opened the door before I rang and told me to come in and wait. Miss Stein would be down at any moment. It was before noon but the maidservant poured me a glass of *eau-de-vie,* put it in my hand and winked happily. The colorless liquid felt good on my tongue and it was still in my mouth when I heard someone speaking to Miss Stein as I had never heard one person speak to another; never, anywhere, ever. Then Miss Stein's voice came pleading and begging, saying, "Don't, pussy. Don't. Don't, please don't. Please don't, pussy."
>
> I swallowed the drink and put the glass down on the table and started for the door. The maidservant shook her finger at me and whispered, "Don't go. She'll be right down."
>
> "I have to go," I said and tried not to hear any more as I left but it was still going on and the only way I could not hear it was to be gone. It was bad to hear and the answers were worse. . . .
>
> That was the way it finished for me, stupidly enough. . . . She got to look like a Roman emperor and that was fine if you liked your women to look like Roman emperors. . . . In the end everyone or not quite everyone made friends again in order not to be stuffy or righteous. But I could never make friends again truly, neither in my heart nor in my head. When you cannot make friends any more in your head is the worst. But it was more complicated than that.[17]

Indeed it is more complicated than that. As we shall see if we keep Ernest Hemingway and Gertrude Stein in mind while we consider another vignette about a man confronting the female voice. This one is from the 7th century BC. It is a lyric fragment of the archaic poet Alkaios of Lesbos. Like Ernest Hemingway, Alkaios was an expatriate writer. He had been expelled from his home city of Mytilene for political insurgency and his poem is a lonely and demoralized lament from exile. Like Hemingway, Alkaios eptomizes his feelings of alienation in the image of himself as a man stranded in an anteroom of high culture and subjected to a disturbing din of women's voices from the room next door:

> . . . wretched I
> exist with wilderness as my lot
> longing to hear the sound of the Assembly

being called, O Agesilaidas,
and the Council.
What my father and the father of my father
grew old enjoying—
among these citizens who wrong one another—
from this I am outcast

an exile on the furthest fringes of things, like Onomaklees
here all alone I have set up my house
in the wolfthickets. . . .

. . . I dwell keeping my feet outside of evils

where the Lesbian women in their contests for beauty
come and go with trailing robes
and all around reverberates
an otherworldly echo of women's awful yearly shrieking (*ololygas*). . . .

ἄγνοις . . σβιότοις . . ις ὀ τάλαις ἔγω
ζώω μοῖραν ἔχων ἀγροϊωτίκαν
ἰμέρρων ἀγορας ἄκουσαι
καρυ[ζο]μένας ὦ ('Α)γεσιλαΐδα

καὶ β[ό]λλας· τὰ πάτηρ καὶ πάτερος πάτηρ
κα(γ)γ[ε]γήρασ' ἔχοντες πεδὰ τωνδέων
τὼν [ἀ]λλαλοκάκων πολίταν
ἔγ[ω . ἀ]πὺ τούτων ἀπελήλαμαι

φεύγων ἐσχατίαισ', ὡς δ' 'Ονυμακλέης
ἔνθα[δ'] οἶος ἐοίκησα λυκαιμίαις
. [ ]ον [π]όλεμον· στάσιν γὰρ
πρὸς κρ . [. . . .] . οὐκ † ἄμεινον † ὀννέλην·

.] . [. . .] . [. .] . μακάρων ἐς τέμ[ε]νος θέων
ἐοι[. . . . .] με[λ]αίνας ἐπίβαις χθόνος
χλι . [.] . [.] . [.]ν συνόδοισί μ' αὔταις
οἴκημι κ[ά]κων ἔκτος ἔχων πόδας,

ὄππαι Λ[εσβί]αδες κριννόμεναι φύαν
πώλεντ' ἐλκεσίπεπλοι, περὶ δὲ βρέμει
ἄχω θεσπεσία γυναίκων
ἴρα[ς ὀ]λολύγας ἐνιαυσίας . . . .[18]

This is a poem of radical loneliness, which Alkaios emphasizes with an oxymoron. "All alone (*oios*) I have set up my household (*eoikesa*)" he says (at verse 10), but this wording would make little sense to a 7th-century BC ear. The verb (*eoikesa*) is made from the noun *oikos,* which denotes the whole relational complex of spaces, objects, kinsmen, servants, animals, rituals and emotions that constitute life within a family within a *polis*. A man all alone cannot constitute an *oikos*.

Alkaios' oxymoronic condition is reinforced by the kind of creatures that surround him. Wolves and women have replaced "the fathers of my fathers." The wolf is a conventional symbol of marginality in Greek poetry. The wolf is an outlaw. He lives beyond the boundary of usefully cultivated and inhabited space marked off as the *polis,* in that blank no man's land called *to apeiron* ("the unbounded"). Women, in the ancient view, share this territory spiritually and metaphorically in virtue of a "natural" female affinity for all that is raw, formless and in need of the civilizing hand of man. So for example in the document cited by Aristotle that goes by the name of The Pythagorean Table of Opposites, we find the attributes curving, dark, secret, evil, ever-moving, not self-contained and lacking its own boundaries aligned with Female and set over against straight, light, honest, good, stable, self-contained and firmly bounded on the Male side (Aristotle, *Metaphysics*).[19]

I do not imagine that these polarities or their hierarchization is news to you, now that classical historians and feminists have spent the last ten or fifteen years codifying the various arguments with which ancient Greek thinkers convinced themselves that women belong to a different race than men. But it interests me that the radical otherness of the female is experienced by Alkaios, as also by Ernest Hemingway, in the form of women's voices uttering sounds that men find bad to hear. Why is female sound bad to hear? The sound that Alkaios hears is that of the local Lesbian women who are conducting beauty contests and making the air reverberate with their yelling. These beauty contests of the Lesbian women are known to us from a notice in the Iliadic scholia which indicates they were an annual event performed probably in honour of Hera. Alkaios mentions the beauty contests in order to remark on their prodigious noise level and, by so doing, draws his poem into a ringcomposition. The poem begins with the urbane and orderly sound of a herald summoning male citizens to their rational civic business in the Assembly and the Council. The poem ends with an otherworldly echo of women shrieking in the wolfthickets. Moreover, the women are uttering a particular kind of shriek, the *ololyga*. This is a ritual shout peculiar to females.[20] It is a highpitched piercing cry uttered at certain climactic moments in ritual practice (e.g., at the moment when a victim's throat is slashed during sacrifice) or at climactic moments in real life (e.g., at the birth of a child) and also a common feature of women's festivals. The *ololyga* with its cognate verb *ololyzo* is one of a family of words, including *eleleu* with its cognate verb *elelizo* and *alala* with its cognate verb *alalazo,* probably of Indo-European origin and obviously of onomatopoeic derivation.[21] These words do not signify anything except their own sound. The sound represents a cry of either intense pleasure or intense pain.[22] To utter such cries is a specialized female function. When Alkaios finds himself surrounded by the sound of the *ololyga* he is telling us that he is completely and genuinely out of bounds. No man would make such sound. No proper civic space would contain it unregulated. The female festivals in which such ritual cries were heard were generally not permitted to be held within the city limits but were relegated to suburban areas like the mountains, the beach or the rooftops of houses where women could disport themselves without contaminating the ears or civic space of men. To be exposed to such sound is for Alkaios a condition of political nakedness as alarming as that of his archetype Odysseus, who awakens with no clothes on in a thicket on the island of Phaiakia in the sixth book of Homer's *Odyssey,* surrounded by the shrieking of women. "What a hullabaloo of females comes around me!" Odysseus exclaims[23] and goes on to wonder what sort of savages or supernatural beings can be making such a racket. The savages of course turn out to be Nausikaa and her girlfriends playing soccer on the riverbank, but what is interesting in this scenario is Odysseus' automatic association of disorderly female sound with wild space, with savagery and the supernatural. Nausikaa and her friends are shortly compared by Homer to the wild girls who roam the mountains in attendance upon Artemis,[24] a goddess herself notorious for the sounds that she makes—if we may judge from her Homeric epithets. Artemis is called *keladeine,* derived from the noun *kelados* which means a loud roaring noise as of wind or rushing water or the tumult of battle. Artemis is also called *iocheaira* which is usually etymologized to mean "she who pours forth arrows" (from *ios* meaning "arrow") but could just as well come from the exclamatory sound *io* and mean "she who pours forth the cry IO!"[25]

Greek women of the archaic and classical periods were not encouraged to pour forth unregulated cries of any kind within the civic space of the *polis* or within earshot of men. Indeed masculinity in such a culture defines itself by its different use of sound. Verbal continence is an essential feature of the masculine virtue of *sophrosyne* ("prudence, soundness of mind, moderation, temperance, self-control") that organizes most patriarchal thinking on ethical or emotional matters. Woman as a species is frequently said to lack the ordering principle of *sophrosyne*. Freud formulates the double standard succinctly in a remark to a colleague: "A thinking man is his own legislator and confessor, and obtains his own absolution, but the woman . . . does not have the measure of ethics in herself. She can only act if she keeps within the limits of morality, following what society has established as fitting."[26] So too, ancient discussions of the virtue of *sophrosyne demonstrate clearly that, where it is applied to women, this word has a different definition than for men.*[27] *Female sophrosyne* is coextensive with female obedience to male direction and rarely means more than chastity. When it does mean more, the allusion is often to sound. A husband exhorting his wife or concubine to *sophrosyne* is likely to mean "Be quiet!"[28] The Pythagorean heroine Timyche who bit off her tongue rather than say the wrong thing is praised as an exception to the female rule.[29] In general the women of classical literature are a species given to disorderly and uncontrolled outflow of sound—to shrieking, wailing, sobbing, shrill lament, loud laughter, screams of pain or of pleasure and eruptions of raw emotion in general. As Euripides puts it, "For it is woman's inborn pleasure always to have her current emotions coming up to her mouth and out through her tongue" (*Andromache*).[30] When a man lets his current emotions come up to his mouth and out through his tongue he is thereby feminized, as Herakles at the end of the *Trachiniai* agonizes to find himself "sobbing like a girl, whereas before I used to follow my difficult course without a groan but now in pain I am discovered a woman."[31]

It is a fundamental assumption of these gender stereotypes that a man in his proper condition of *sophrosyne* should be able to dissociate himself from his own emotions and so control their sound. It is a corollary assumption that man's proper civic responsibility towards woman is to control her sound for her insofar as she cannot control it herself. We see a summary moment of such masculine benevolence in Homer's *Odyssey* in Book 22 when the old woman Eurykleia enters the dining hall to find Odysseus caked in blood and surrounded by dead suitors. Eurykleia lifts her head and opens her mouth to utter an *ololyga*. Whereupon Odysseus reaches out a hand and closes her mouth saying, *ou themis:* "It is not permitted for you to scream just now. Rejoice inwardly. . . ."[32]

Closing women's mouths was the object of a complex array of legislation and convention in preclassical and classical Greece, of which the best documented examples are Solon's sumptuary laws and the core concept is Sophokles' blanket statement, "Silence is the *kosmos* [good order] of women."[33] The sumptuary laws enacted by Solon in the 6th century BC had as their effect, Plutarch tells us, "to forbid all the disorderly and barbarous excesses of women in their festivals, processions and funeral rites."[34] The main responsibility for funeral lament had belonged to women from earliest Greek times. Already in Homer's *Iliad* we see the female Trojan captives in Achilles' camp compelled to wail over Patroklos.[35] Yet lawgivers of the 6th and 5th centuries like Solon were at pains to restrict these female outpourings to a minimum of sound and emotional display.

The official rhetoric of the lawgivers is instructive. It tends to denounce bad sound as political disease (*nosos*) and speaks of the need to purify civic spaces of such pollution. Sound itself is regarded as the means of purification as well as of pollution. So for example the lawgiver Charondas, who laid down laws for the city of Katana in Sicily, prefaced his legal code with a ceremonial public *katharsis*. This took the form of an incantation meant to cleanse the citizen body of evil ideas or criminal intent and to prepare a civic space for the legal *katharsis* that followed. In his law code Charondas, like Solon, was concerned to regulate female noise and turned attention to the ritual funeral lament. Laws were passed specifying the location, time, duration, personnel, choreography, musical content and verbal content of the women's funeral lament on the grounds that these "harsh and barbaric sounds" were a stimulus to "disorder and licence" (as Plutarch puts it).[36] Female sound was judged to arise in craziness and to generate craziness.

We detect a certain circularity in the reasoning here. If women's public utterance is perpetually enclosed within cultural institutions like the ritual lament, if women are regularly reassigned to the expression of nonrational sounds like the *ololyga* and raw emotion in general, then the so-called "natural" tendency of the female to shrieking, wailing, weeping, emotional display and oral disorder cannot help but become a self-fulfilling prophecy. But circularity is not the most ingenious thing about this reasoning. We should look a little more closely at the ideology that underlies male abhorrence of female sound. And it becomes important at this point to distinguish sound from language.

For the formal definition of human nature preferred by patriarchal culture is one based on articulation of sound. As Aristotle says, any animal can make noises to register pleasure or pain. But what differentiates man from beast, and civilization from the wilderness, is the use of rationally articulated speech: *logos*.[37] From such a prescription for humanity follow severe rules for what constitutes human *logos*. When the wife of Alexander Graham Bell, a woman who had been deafened in childhood and knew how to lipread but not how to talk very well, asked him to teach her sign language, Alexander replied, "The use of sign language is pernicious. For the only way by which language can be thoroughly mastered is by using it for the communication of thought without translation into any other language."[38] Alexander Graham Bell's wife, whom he had married the day after he patented the telephone, never did learn sign language. Or any other language.

What is it that is pernicious about sign language? To a husband like Alexander Graham Bell, as to a patriarchal social order like that of classical Greece, there is something disturbing or abnormal about the use of signs to transcribe upon the outside of the body a meaning from inside the body which does not pass through the control point of *logos,* a meaning which is not subject to the mechanism of dissociation that the Greeks called *sophrosyne* or self-control. Sigmund Freud applied the name "hysteria" to this process of transcription when it occurred in female patients whose tics and neuralgias and convulsions and paralyses and eating disorders and spells of blindness could be read, in his theory, as a direct translation into somatic terms of psychic events within the woman's body.[39] Freud conceived his own therapeutic task as the rechannelling of these hysteric signs into rational discourse.[40] Herodotos tells us of a priestess of Athene in Pedasa who did not use speech to prophesy but would grow a beard whenever she saw misfortune coming upon her community.[41] Herodotos does not register any surprise at the "somatic compliance" (as Freud would call it) of this woman's prophetic body nor call her condition pathological. But Herodotos was a practical person, less concerned to discover pathologies in his historical subjects than to congratulate them for putting "otherness" to cultural use. And the anecdote does give us a strong image of how ancient culture went about constructing the "otherness" of the female. Woman is that creature who puts the inside on the outside. By projections and leakages of all kinds—somatic, vocal, emotional, sexual—females expose or expend what should be kept in. Females blurt out a direct translation of what should be formulated indirectly. There is a story told about the wife of Pythagoras, that she once uncovered her arm while out of doors and someone commented, "Nice arm," to which she responded, "Not public property!" Plutarch's comment on this story is: "The arm of a virtuous woman should not be public property, nor her speech neither, and she should as modestly guard against exposing her voice to outsiders as she would guard against stripping off her clothes. For in her voice as she is blabbering away can be read her emotions, her character and her physical condition."[42] In spite of herself, Plutarch's woman has a voice that acts like a sign language, exposing her inside facts. Ancient physiologists from Aristotle through the early Roman empire tell us that a man can know from the sound of a woman's voice private data like whether or not she is menstruating, whether or not she has had sexual experience.[43] Although these are useful things to know, they may be bad to hear or make men uncomfortable. What is pernicious about sign language is that it permits a direct continuity between inside and outside. Such continuity is abhorrent to the male nature. The masculine virtue of *sophrosyne* or self-control aims to obstruct this continuity, to dissociate the outside surface of a man from what is going on inside him. Man breaks continuity by interposing *logos*—whose most important censor is the rational articulation sound.

Every sound we make is a bit of autobiography. It has a totally private interior yet its trajectory is public. A piece of inside projected to the outside. The censorship of such projections is a task of patriarchal culture that (as we have seen) divides humanity into two species: those who can censor themselves and those who cannot.

In order to explore some of the implications of this division let us consider how Plutarch depicts the two species in his essay "On Talkativeness."

To exemplify the female species in its use of sound Plutarch tells the story of a politician's wife who is tested by her husband. The politician makes up a crazy story and tells it to his wife as a secret early one morning. "Now keep your mouth closed about this," he warns her. The wife immediately relates the secret to her maidservant. "Now keep your mouth closed about this," she tells the maidservant, who immediately relates it to the whole town and before midmorning the politician himself receives his own story back again. Plutarch concludes this anecdote by saying, "The husband had taken precautions and protective measures in order to test his wife, as one might test a cracked or leaky vessel by filling it not with oil or wine but with water."[44] Plutarch pairs this anecdote with a story about masculine speech acts. It is a description of a friend of Solon's named Anacharsis:

> Anacharsis who had dined with Solon and was resting after dinner, was seen pressing his left hand on his sexual parts and his right hand on his mouth: for he believed that the tongue requires a more powerful restraint. And he was right. It would not be easy to count as many men lost through incontinence in amorous pleasures as cities and empires ruined through revelation of a secret.[45]

In assessing the implications of the gendering of sound for a society like that of the ancient Greeks, we have to take seriously the connexion Plutarch makes between verbal and sexual continence, between mouth and genitals. Because that connexion turns out to be a very different matter for men than for women. The masculine virtue of self-censorship with which Anacharsis responds to impulses from inside himself is shown to be simply unavailable to the female nature.

Plutarch reminds us a little later in the essay that perfect *sophrosyne* is an attribute of the god Apollo whose epithet Loxias means that he is a god of few words and concise expression, not one who runs off at the mouth.[46] Now when a woman runs off at the mouth there is far more at stake than waste of words: the image of the leaky water jar with which Plutarch concludes his first anecdote is one of the commonest figures in ancient literature for the representation of female sexuality.

The forms and contexts of this representation (the leaky jar of female sexuality) have been studied at length by other scholars including me,[47] so let us pass directly to the heart, or rather the mouth, of the matter. It is an axiom of ancient Greek and Roman medical theory and anatomical discussion that a woman has two mouths.[48] The orifice through which vocal activity takes place and the orifice through which sexual activity takes place are both denoted by the word *stoma* in Greek (*os* in Latin) with the addition of adverbs *ano* or *kato* to differentiate upper mouth from lower mouth. Both the vocal and the genital mouth are connected to the body by a neck (*auchen* in Greek, *cervix* in Latin). Both mouths provide access to a hollow cavity which is guarded by lips that are best kept closed. The ancient medical writers apply not only homologous terms but also parallel medications to upper and lower mouths in certain cases of uterine malfunction. They note with interest, as do many poets and scholiasts, symptoms of physiological responsion between upper and lower mouth, for example that an excess or blockage of blood in the uterus will evidence itself as strangulation or loss of voice,[49] that too much vocal exercise results in loss of menses,[50] that defloration causes a woman's neck to enlarge and her voice to deepen.[51]

"With a high pure voice because she has not yet been acted upon by the bull," is how Aiskhylos describes his Iphigeneia (*Agamemnon*).[52] The changed voice and enlarged throat of the sexually initiated female are an upward projection of irrevocable changes at the lower mouth. Once a woman's sexual life begins, the lips of the uterus are never completely closed again—except on one occasion, as the medical writers explain: in his treatise on gynecology Soranos describes the sensations that a woman experiences during fruitful sexual intercourse. At the moment of conception, the Hellenistic doctor Soranos alleges, the woman has a shivering sensation and the perception that the mouth of her uterus closes upon the seed.[53] This closed mouth, and the good silence of conception that it protects and signifies, provides the model of decorum for the upper mouth as well. Sophokles' frequently cited dictum "Silence is the *kosmos* of women" has its medical analog in women's amulets from antiquity which picture a uterus equipped with a lock at the mouth.

When it is not locked the mouth may gape open and let out unspeakable things. Greek myth, literature and cult show traces of cultural anxiety about such female ejaculation. For example there is the story of Medusa who, when her head was cut off by Perseus, gave birth to a son and a flying horse through her neck.[54] Or again that restless and loquacious nymph Echo, surely the most mobile female in Greek myth. When Sophokles calls her "the girl with no door on her mouth" we might wonder which mouth he means. Especially since Greek legend marries Echo off in the end to the god Pan whose name implies her conjugal union with every living thing.

We should also give some consideration to that bizarre and variously explained religious practice called *aischrologia*. *Aischrologia* means "saying ugly things." Certain women's festivals included an interval in which women shouted abusive remarks or obscenities or dirty jokes at one another. Historians of religion classify these rituals of bad sound either as some Frazerian species of fertility magic or as a type of coarse but cheering buffoonery in which (as Walter Burkert says) "antagonism between the sexes is played up and finds release."[55] But the fact remains that in general men were not welcome at these rituals and Greek legend contains more than a few cautionary tales of men castrated, dismembered or killed when they blundered into them.[56] These stories suggest a backlog of sexual anger behind the bland face of religious buffoonery. Ancient society was happy to have women drain off such unpleasant tendencies and raw emotion into a leakproof ritual container. The strategy involved here is a kathartic one, based on a sort of psychological division of labour between the sexes, such as [pseudo]Demosthenes mentions in a reference to the Athenian ritual called *Choes*. The ceremony of *Choes* took place on the second day of the Dionysian festival of Anthesteria.[57] It featured a competition between celebrants to drain an oversize jug of wine and concluded with a symbolic (or perhaps not) act of sexual union between the god Dionysos and a representative woman of the community. It is this person to whom Demosthenes refers, saying "She is the woman who discharges the unspeakable things on behalf of the city."[58]

Let us dwell for a moment on this ancient female task of discharging unspeakable things on behalf of the city, and on the structures that the city sets up to contain such speech.

A ritual structure like the *aischrologia* raises some difficult questions of definition. For it collapses into a single kathartic activity two different aspects of sound production. We have noticed this combinatory tactic already throughout most of the ancient and some of the modern discussions of voice: female sound is bad to hear *both* because the quality of a woman's voice is objectionable *and* because woman uses her voice to say what should not be said. When these two aspects are blurred together, some important questions about the distinction between essential and constructed characteristics of human nature recede into circularity. Nowadays, sex difference in language is a topic of diverse research and unresolved debate. The sounds made by women are said to have different inflectional patterns, different ranges of intonation, different syntactic preferences, different semantic fields, different diction, different narrative textures, different behavioural accoutrements, different contextual pressures than the sounds that men make.[59] Tantalizing vestiges of ancient evidence for such difference may be read from, e.g., passing references in Aristophanes to a "woman's language" that a man can learn or imitate if he wants to (*Thesmophoriazousai*),[60] or from the conspicuously onomatopoeic construction of female cries like *ololuga* and female names like Gorgo, Baubo, Echo, Syrinx, Eileithyia.[61] But in general, no clear account of the ancient facts can be extracted from strategically blurred notions like the homology of female mouth and female genitals, or tactically blurred activities like the ritual of the *aischrologia*. What does emerge is a consistent paradigm of response to otherness of voice. It is a paradigm that forms itself as *katharsis*.

As such, the ancient Greek ritual of *aischrologia* bears some resemblance to the procedure developed by Sigmund Freud and his colleague Josef Breuer for treatment of hysterical women. In *Case Studies on Hysteria* Freud and Breuer use the term "katharsis" and also the term "talking cure" of this revolutionary therapy. In Freud's theory the hysterical patients are women who have bad memories or ugly emotions trapped inside them like a pollution. Freud and Breuer find themselves able to drain off this pollution by inducing the women under hypnosis to speak unspeakable things. Hypnotized women produce some remarkable sounds. One of the case studies described by Freud can at first only clack like a hen; another insists on speaking English although she was Viennese; another uses what Freud calls "paraphrastic jargon."[62] But all are eventually channelled by the psychoanalyst into connected narrative and rational exegesis of their hysteric symptoms. Whereupon, both Freud and Breuer claim, the symptoms disappear—cleansed by this simple kathartic ritual of draining off the bad sound of unspeakable things.

Here is how Josef Breuer describes his interaction with the patient who goes by the pseudonym Anna O.:

> . . . . I used to visit her in the evening, when I knew I should find her in her hypnosis, and then I relieved her of the whole stock of imaginative products which she had accumulated since my last visit. It was essential that this should be effected completely if good results were to follow. When this was done she became perfectly calm, and next day she would be agreeable, easy to manage, industrious and even cheerful. . . . She aptly described this procedure as a "talking cure," while she referred to it jokingly as "chimney sweeping."[63]

Whether we call it chimney sweeping or *aischrologia* or ritual funeral lament or a hullabaloo of females or having a laugh like a beefsteak, the same paradigm of response is obvious. As if the entire female gender were a kind of collective bad memory of unspeakable things, patriarchal order like a well-intentioned psychoanalyst seems to conceive its therapeutic responsibility as the channelling of this bad sound into politically appropriate containers. Both the upper and the lower female mouth apparently stand in need of such controlling action. Freud mentions shyly in a footnote to *Case Studies on Hysteria* that Josef Breuer had to suspend his analytic relationship with Anna O. because "she suddenly made manifest to Breuer the presence of a strongly unanalyzed positive transference of an unmistakably sexual nature."[64] Not until 1932 did Freud reveal (in a letter to a colleague)[65] what really happened between Breuer and Anna O. It was on the evening of his last interview with her that Breuer entered Anna's apartment to find her on the floor contorted by abdominal pain. When he asked her what was wrong she answered that she was about to give birth to his child. It was this "untoward event" as Freud calls it that caused Breuer to hold back the publication of *Case Studies on Hysteria* from 1881 to 1895 and led him ultimately to abandon collaborating with Freud. Even the talking cure must fall silent when both female mouths try to speak at the same time.

It is confusing and embarrassing to have two mouths. Genuine *kakophony* is the sound produced by them. Let us consider one more example from antiquity of female *kakophony* at its most confusing and embarrassing. There is a group of terracotta statues recovered from Asia Minor and dated to the 4th century BC which depict the female body in an alarmingly shortcircuited form.[66] Each of these statues is a woman who consists of almost nothing but her two mouths. The two mouths are welded together into an inarticulate body mass which excludes other anatomical function. Moreover the position of the two mouths is reversed. The upper mouth for talking is placed at the bottom of the statue's belly. The lower or genital mouth gapes open on top of the head. Iconographers identify this monster with the old woman named Baubo[67] who figures in Greek legend as an allomorph of the old woman Iambe (in the Demeter myth) and is a sort of patron saint of the ritual of the *aischrologia*. Baubo's name has a double significance; according to *LSJ* the noun *baubo* is used as a synonym for *koilia* (which denotes the female uterus) but as a piece of sound it derives from *baubau*, the onomatopoeic Greek word for a dog's bark.[68] The mythic action of Baubo is also significantly double. Like the old woman Iambe, Baubo is credited in legend with the twofold gesture of pulling up her clothes to reveal her genitalia and also shouting out obscene language or jokes. The shouting of Baubo provides one aetiology for the ritual of the *aischrologia;* her action of genital exposure may also have come over into cult as a ritual action called the *anasyrma* (the "pulling up" of clothing).[69] If so, we may understand this action as a kind of visual or gestural noise, projected outward upon circumstances to change or deflect them, in the manner of an apotropaic utterance. So Plutarch describes the use of the *anasyrma* gesture by women in besieged cites: in order to repel the enemy they stand on the city wall and pull up their clothing to expose unspeakable things.[70] Plutarch praises this action of female self-exposure as an instance of virtue in its context. But woman's allegedly definitive tendency to put the inside on the outside could provoke quite another reaction. The Baubo statues are strong evidence of that reaction. This Baubo presents us with one simple chaotic diagram of an outrageously manipulable female identity. The doubling and interchangeability of mouth engenders a creature in whom sex is cancelled out by sound and sound is cancelled out by sex. This seems a perfect answer to all the questions raised and dangers posed by the confusing and embarrassing continuity of female nature. Baubo's mouths appropriate each other.

Cultural historians disagree on the meaning of these statues. They have no certain information on the gender or intention or state of mind of the people who made them. We can only guess at their purpose as objects or their mood as works of art. Personally I find them as ugly and confusing and almost funny as *Playboy* magazine in its current predilection for placing centrefold photographs of naked women side by side with long intensely empathetic articles about high-profile feminists. This is more than an oxymoron. There is a death of meaning in the collocation of such falsehoods—each of them, the centrefold naked woman and the feminist, a social construct purchased and marketed by *Playboy* magazine to facilitate that fantasy of masculine virtue that the ancient Greeks called *sophrosyne* and Freud renamed repression.

In considering the question, how do our presumptions about gender affect the way we hear sounds? I have cast my net rather wide and have mingled evidence from different periods of time and different forms of cultural expression—in a way that reviewers of my work like to dismiss as ethnographic naïveté. I think there is a place for naïveté in ethnography, at the very least as an irritant. Sometimes when I am reading a Greek text I force myself to look up all the words in the dictionary, even the ones I think I know. It is surprising what you learn that way. Some of the words turn out to sound quite different than you thought. Sometimes the way they sound can make you ask questions you wouldn't otherwise ask. Lately I have begun to question the Greek word *sophrosyne*. I wonder about this concept of self-control and whether it really is, as the Greeks believed, an answer to most questions of human goodness and dilemmas of civility. I wonder if there might not be another idea of human order than repression, another notion of human virtue than self-control, another kind of human self than one based on dissociation of inside and outside. Or indeed, another human essence than self.

Endnotes

1. *Physiognomics,* 807a.
2. *Physiognomics,* 813a. On *kinaidos* see Aiskhines 1.131 and 2.99; Dover (1975), 17, 75; M. W. Gleason (1990), 401; I am indebted to Maud Gleason also for allowing me to preview a chapter ("The Role of the Voice in the Maintenance of Gender Boundaries") of her book on self-presentation in the Second Sophistic, *Making Men: Sophists and Self-Presentation in Ancient Rome.*
3. Aristophanes, *Ekklesiazousai,* 113–114.
4. Aristotle, *On the Generation of Animals,* 787b–788.
5. Oribasios, 6; Gleason (1994), 12.
6. A. Raphael, *The Observer,* October 7, 1979.
7. S. Rogers in S. Ardener (1981), 59.
8. T. Howe (1954), 209; J.-P. Vernant (1991), 117.
9. *Eumenides,* 117, 131.
10. *Odyssey,* 4.275.
11. Aiskhylos, *Agamemnon,* 1213–1214.
12. *Homeric Hymn to Aphrodite,* 18–20.
13. *Iliad,* 14.216.
14. On Iambe see M. Olender (1990), 85–90 and references.
15. *Philoktetes,* 188.
16. M. D. Luhan (1935), 324.
17. E. Hemingway (1964), 118.
18. fr. 130 Lobel.
19. Aristotle, *Metaphysics,* 986a22.
20. S. Eitrem (1919), III, 44–53 assembles the pertinent texts.
21. E. Boisacq (1907), 698.
22. L. Gernet (1983), 248 and n. 8.
23. *Od.* 6. 122.
24. *Od.* 9. 105–6.
25. So Gernet (1983), 249–250 following Ehrlich (1910), 48.
26. Letter to E. Silberstein cited by Grosskurth (1980), 889.
27. H. North (1966), see especially 1, 22, 37, 59, 206.

28. *E.g.* Sophokles, *Ajax,* 586.
29. Iamblichos, *Life of Pythagoras,* 31, 194.
30. *Andromache,* 94–5.
31. 1070–5.
32. *od.* 22. 405-6.
33. Cited by Aristotle, *Politics,* 1, 1260a30.
34. *Life of Solon,* 21 = *Moralia,* 65b.
35. 18.339.
36. *Ibid.,* 12.5 and 21.4. I learn from Marilyn Katz that there is serious contemporary debate about Jewish women praying aloud (i.e., reading from the Torah) at the Western Wall in Jerusalem: "The principal objection that I have heard has to do with the men's enforced exposure to *kol ishah* (female voice) from which they are normally expected to be protected, for a vast array of reasons articulated by rabbis in the Talmud and elsewhere, including sexual temptation."
37. *Politics,* 1253a.
38. This anecdote formed part of a lecture A. G. B. delivered to the Social Science Association, Boston, December 1871.
39. S. Freud and J. Breuer (1965).
40. "We found that each individual hysterical symptom immediately and permanently disappeared when we had succeeded in bringing clearly to light the memory of the event by which it was provoked and . . . when the patient had described that event in the greatest possible detail and had put the affect into words." Freud goes on to say that the psychotherapeutic method works "by allowing strangulated affect to find a way out through speech" (*Ibid.,* 6, 253).
41. 1.75.
42. *Life of Pythagoras,* 7 = *Moralia,* 142d; Gleason, 65.
43. Aristotle, *History of Animals,* 581a31–b5; Suidas *s.v. Diagnomon;* Gleason 53; A. Hanson and D. Armstrong (1986), 97–100; A. Hanson (1990), 328–329 and references.
44. *On Talkativeness.* 7 = *Moralia,* 507b–d.
45. *Ibid.,* 7 = *Moralia,* 505a.
46. *Ibid.,* 17 = *Moralia,* 511b6–10.
47. The logic of the representation has obviously to do with male observation of the mysteriously unfailing moistures of female physiology and also with a prevailing ancient medical conception of the female uterus as an upside down jar. See Carson (1990); A. Hanson (1990), 325–327; G. Sissa (1990), 125–157.
48. Hippokrates, *Diseases of Women,* 2.137, 8.310.5 (Littré); Galen, *On the*

Usefulness of the Parts, 15.3; Hanson (1990), 321–329; Olender (1990), 104–105; Sissa (1990), 5, 53–66, 70, 166–168.

49. Galen, *On Generation,* 15.2–3; Hanson (1990), 328.
50. Soranos, *Gynaikeia;* 1.4.22; Gleason, 122.
51. Aiskhylos, *Agamemnon,* 244; Hanson (1990), 329–332; Hanson and Armstrong (1986).
52. *Agamemnon,* 244.
53. Soranos, *Gynaikeia,* 1.44; *Corpus Medicorum Graecorum,* 4.3.1.9–11 (Ilberg): Hanson (1990), 315, 321–322.
54. Hesiod, *Theogony,* 280–281; Wasson *et al.* (1978), 120.
55. "The Greek evidence points most conspicuously to the absurdity and buffoonery of the whole affair: there is a conscious descent to the lower classes and the lower parts of the anatomy. . . .": W. Burkert (1985), 105.
56. Euripides, *Bakkhai;* M. Detienne and J.-P. Vernant (1979), 184–186; F. Zeitlin (1982), 146–153.
57. On the Anthesteria see Parke (1977), 107–113; Burkert (1985), 239.
58. 59.73.
59. See, *e.g.,* Adler (1978); Cixous (1981); Gatens (1991); especially 6–84; Irigaray (1990); Kramarae (1981); Lakoff (1975); Sapir (1949); Spender (1985).
60. Aristophanes, *Thesmophoriazousai,* 192, 267.
61. See also Zeitlin (1985) on the feminization of the male in Greek tragedy.
62. Freud and Breuer (1966), 5–17, 29.
63. *Ibid.,* 30.
64. *Ibid.,* 40 n. 1.
65. Gay (1988), 67.
66. Olender (1990) and plates.
67. H. Diels made the identification (1907); on Baubo see further A. N. Athanassakis (1976); Burkert (1985), 368; Devereux (1983); Graf (1974), 169, 171; Lobeck (1829); Olender (1990).
68. Olender suggests another explanation, associated with nursing an infant: (1990), 97–99 and references.
69. Graf (1974), 169, 195; Olender (1990), 93–95.
70. *On the Virtue of Women,* 5.9 = *Moralia,* 532f.

Bibliography

Adler, M. K. (1978), *Sex Differences in Human Speech,* Hamburg.
Alexiou, M. (1974), *The Ritual Lament in Greek Tradition,* Oxford.
Ardener, S. (1981), *Women and Space,* London.
Athanassakis, A. N. (1976), "Music and Ritual in Primitive Eleusis," *Platon* 28, 86–105.
Boisacq, E. (1907), *Dictionnaire étymologique de la langue grecque,* Paris & Heidelberg.
Burguière, P., ed. (1988), *Soranus. Maladies des Femmes I,* Paris.
Burkert, W. (1983), *Homo Necans,* translated by P. Bing, Berkeley.
———. (1985), *Greek Religion,* translated by J. Raffan, Cambridge, Mass.
Cameron, A. and A. Kuhrt (1983), *Images of Women in Antiquity,* London.
Cameron, D. (1990), *The Feminist Critique of Language: A Reader,* London & New York.
Carson, A. (1990), "Putting Her in Her Place: Woman as Dirt in Ancient Society," 135–170 in Zeitlin (1990).
Channon, Sir H. (1967), *Chips: The Diaries of Sir Henry Channon,* London.
Cixous, H. (1981), "Castration or Decapitation?," *Signs* 7, 27–39.
Dean-Jones, L. (1989), "Menstrual Bleeding According to the Hippocraticis and Aristotle," *Transactions & Proceedings of the American Philological Association* 119, 177–192.
Detienne, M. and J.-P. Vernant (1979), *La cuisine du sacrifice en pays grec,* Paris.
Devereux, G. (1983), *Baubo: La vulve mythique,* Paris.
Diels, H. (1907), "Arcana cerealia," 3–14 in *Miscellanea di archeologia, storia e filologia dedicata al Professore A. Salinas,* Palermo.
Doane, M. A. (1986), "The Clinical Eye: Medical Discourses in the Woman's Film of the 1940's" in Suleiman (1986).
Dover, Sir K. J. (1975), *Greek Homosexuality,* Oxford.
Ehrlich, H. (1910), *Zur indogermanischen Sprachgeschichte,* Konigsberg.
Eitrem, S. (1919), *Beiträge zur griechischen Religionsgeschichte,* 3 vols., Kristiana.
Freud, S. (1925), "A Mythical Parallel to a Visual Obsession" 4, 345–346, in *Collected Papers,* translated by J. Strachey, London.
Freud, S. and J. Breuer (1966), *Case Studies on Hysteria,* translated by J. Strachey, New York.
Gatens, M. (1991), *Feminism and Philosophy,* Cambridge.
Gay, P. (1988), *Freud: A Life for our Time,* New York.

Gernet, L. (1953), "Dionysos et la religion Dionysique," *Revue des études grecques* 66, 377–395 = *Anthropologie de la Grèce antique,* Paris 1968, 63–89.
——— (1983), *Les Grecs sans miracle,* Paris.
Gleason, M. W. (1990), "The Semiotics of Gender: Physiognomics and Self-Fashioning in the Second Century C.E.," 389–415, in Zeitlin (1990).
——— (1994), *Making Men: Sophists and Self-Presentation in Ancient Rome,* Princeton.
Graf, F. (1974), *Eleusis and die orphische Dichtung: Athens in vorhellenistischer Zeit,* Berlin.
Grosskurth, P. (1980), "Review of R. W. Clarke, *Freud: The Man and the Cause,*" *TLS,* August 8, 887–890.
Hanson, A. (1975), "Hippocrates: Diseases of Women 1," *Signs* 1, 567–584.
——— (1985), "The Women of the Hippocratic Corpus," *Bulletin of the Society of Ancient Medicine,* 13, 5–7.
——— and D. Armstrong (1986), "The Virgin's Neck and Voice: Aeschylus, *Agamemnon* 245 and Other Texts," *Bulletin of the Institute of Classical Studies,* 97 sqq.
——— (1988), "Diseases of Women" in Burguière (1988).
——— (1990), "The Medical Writers' Woman," 308–335, in Zeitlin (1990).
Hemingway, E. (1964), *A Moveable Feast,* New York.
Hippocrates, *Oeuvres complètes d'Hippocrate,* ed. E. Littré, 10 vols. , Paris 1839–1861; repr. Amsterdam (1962).
Holst-Warhaft, D. (1992), *Dangerous Voices,* New York.
Howe, T. (1954), "The Origin and Function of the Gorgon Head," *American Journal of Archaeology* 58, 209–221.
Irigaray, L. (1990), *Sexes et genres à travers les langues,* Paris.
King, H. (1983), "Bound to Bleed: Artemis and Greek Women," 109–127, in Cameron (1983).
Kramarae, C. (1981), *Women and Men Speaking,* Rowley, Mass.
Lakoff, R. (1975), *Language and Woman's Place,* New York.
Lobeck, C. A. (1829), *Aglaophamus sive de Theologiae Mysticae Graecorum Causis,* 3 vols., Konigsberg.
Lobel, E. and D. L. Page (1955), *Poetarum Lesbiorum Fragmenta,* Oxford.
Luhan, M. D. (1935), *Intimate Memoirs,* 2 vols., New York.
MacKinnon, C. (1987), *Feminism Unmodified: Discourses on Life and Law,* Cambridge, Mass.
North, H. (1966), *Sophrosyne,* Ithaca.

Olender, M. (1990), "Aspects of Baubo: Ancient Texts and Contexts," 83–107, in Zeitlin (1990).

Oribasios, *Collectionum medicarum reliquiae,* ed. J. Raeder, 4 vols. (*Corpus Medicorum Graecorum* 6.1.1–2 and 2.1–2, Leipzig 1928–1933).

Parke, H. W. (1979), *Festivals of the Athenians,* London.

Raphael, A. (1979), *The Observer,* October 7.

Sapir, E. (1949), *Selected Writings on Language, Culture and Personality,* Berkeley.

Sissa, G. (1990), *Greek Virginity,* translated by A. Goldhammer, Cambridge, Mass.

Soranos, *Sorani Gynaeciorum Libri IV,* ed. J. Ilberg (*Corpus Medicorum Graecorum* 4, Berlin 1927).

——— *Soranus' Gynecology* (1956), translated by O. Temkin, Baltimore.

Spender, D. (1985), *Man Made Language,* London.

Suleiman, S. R. (1986), *The Feminine Body in Western Culture,* Cambridge, Mass.

Vernant, J.-P. (1982), *The Origins of Greek Thought,* Ithaca.

——— (1991), *Mortals and Immortals,* ed. F. Zeitlin, Princeton.

Wasson, R. and C. P. Ruck and A. Hoffman (1982), *The Road to Eleusis,* New York.

Zeitlin, F. (1982), "Cultic Models of the Female," *Arethusa* 15, 129–137.

——— (1985), "Playing the Other: Theater, Theatricality and the Feminine in Greek Drama," *Representations* 11, 63–94.

——— *et al.*, eds. (1990), *Before Sexuality,* Princeton.

New Directions Paperbooks—a partial listing

César Aira
An Episode in the Life of a Landscape Painter
Ghosts
The Literary Conference
Will Alexander, The Sri Lankan Loxodrome
Paul Auster, The Red Notebook
Gennady Aygi, Child-and-Rose
Honoré de Balzac, Colonel Chabert
Djuna Barnes, Nightwood
Charles Baudelaire, The Flowers of Evil*
Bei Dao, The Rose of Time: New & Selected Poems*
Nina Berberova, The Ladies From St. Petersburg
Roberto Bolaño, By Night in Chile
Distant Star
Last Evenings on Earth
Nazi Literature in the Americas
The Skating Rink
Jorge Luis Borges, Labyrinths
Seven Nights
Coral Bracho, Firefly Under the Tongue*
Kamau Brathwaite, Ancestors
William Bronk, Selected Poems
Sir Thomas Browne, Urn Burial
Basil Bunting, Complete Poems
Anne Carson, Glass, Irony & God
Horacio Castellanos Moya, Senselessness
Tyrant Memory
Louis-Ferdinand Céline
Death on the Installment Plan
Journey to the End of the Night
René Char, Selected Poems
Inger Christensen, alphabet
Jean Cocteau, The Holy Terrors
Peter Cole, Things on Which I've Stumbled
Maurice Collis, Cortes & Montezuma
Julio Cortázar, Cronopios & Famas
Albert Cossery, A Splendid Conspiracy
Robert Creeley, If I Were Writing This
Life and Death
Guy Davenport, 7 Greeks
Osamu Dazai, The Setting Sun
H.D., Trilogy
Robert Duncan, Groundwork
Selected Poems
Eça de Queirós, The Maias
William Empson, 7 Types of Ambiguity
Shusaku Endo, Deep River
The Samurai
Jenny Erpenbeck, The Old Child
Visitation
Lawrence Ferlinghetti
A Coney Island of the Mind
A Far Rockaway of the Heart
Thalia Field, Bird Lovers, Backyard
F. Scott Fitzgerald, The Crack-Up
On Booze
Forrest Gander, As a Friend
Core Samples From the World
Romain Gary, The Life Before Us (Mme. Rosa)
William Gerhardie, Futility
Henry Green, Pack My Bag
Allen Grossman, Descartes' Loneliness
John Hawkes, The Lime Twig
Second Skin
Felisberto Hernández, Lands of Memory
Hermann Hesse, Siddhartha
Takashi Hiraide
For the Fighting Spirit of the Walnut*
Yoel Hoffman, The Christ of Fish
Susan Howe, My Emily Dickinson
That This
Bohumil Hrabal, I Served the King of England
Ihara Saikaku, The Life of an Amorous Woman
Christopher Isherwood, The Berlin Stories
Fleur Jaeggy, Sweet Days of Discipline
Gustav Janouch, Conversations With Kafka
Alfred Jarry, Ubu Roi
B.S. Johnson, House Mother Normal
Franz Kafka, Amerika: The Man Who Disappeared
Bob Kaufman, Solitudes Crowded With Loneliness
Heinrich von Kleist, Prince Friedrich of Homburg
Laszlo Krasznahorkai
The Melancholy of Resistance
War & War
Mme. de Lafayette, The Princess of Clèves
Lautréamont, Maldoror
Denise Levertov, Selected Poems
Tesserae
Li Po, Selected Poems
Clarice Lispector, The Hour of the Star
Soulstorm
Luljeta Lleshanaku, Child of Nature
Federico García Lorca, Selected Poems*
Three Tragedies
Nathaniel Mackey, Splay Anthem
Stéphane Mallarmé, Selected Poetry and Prose*

Javier Marías, All Souls
A Heart So White
Your Face Tomorrow (3 volumes)
Thomas Merton, New Seeds of Contemplation
The Way of Chuang Tzu
Henri Michaux, Selected Writings
Dunya Mikhail, Diary of a Wave Outside the Sea
Henry Miller, The Air-Conditioned Nightmare
Big Sur & The Oranges of Hieronymus Bosch
The Colossus of Maroussi
Yukio Mishima, Confessions of a Mask
Death in Midsummer
Teru Miyamoto, Kinshu: Autumn Brocade
Eugenio Montale, Selected Poems*
Vladimir Nabokov, Laughter in the Dark
Nikolai Gogol
The Real Life of Sebastian Knight
Pablo Neruda, The Captain's Verses*
Love Poems*
Residence on Earth*
Charles Olson, Selected Writings
George Oppen, New Collected Poems (with CD)
Wilfred Owen, Collected Poems
Michael Palmer, Thread
Nicanor Parra, Antipoems*
Boris Pasternak, Safe Conduct
Kenneth Patchen, The Walking-Away World
Octavio Paz, The Collected Poems 1957–1987*
A Tale of Two Gardens
Victor Pelevin, Omon Ra
Saint-John Perse, Selected Poems
Ezra Pound, The Cantos
New Selected Poems and Translations
Personae
Raymond Queneau, Exercises in Style
Qian Zhongshu, Fortress Besieged
Raja Rao, Kanthapura
Herbert Read, The Green Child
Kenneth Rexroth, Songs of Love, Moon & Wind
Written on the Sky: Poems from the Japanese
Rainer Maria Rilke
Poems from the Book of Hours
The Possibility of Being
Arthur Rimbaud, Illuminations*
A Season in Hell and The Drunken Boat*
Guillermo Rosales, The Halfway House
Evilio Rosero, The Armies
Good Offices
Joseph Roth, The Leviathan
Jerome Rothenberg, Triptych
William Saroyan
The Daring Young Man on the Flying Trapeze
Jean-Paul Sartre, Nausea
The Wall
Delmore Schwartz
In Dreams Begin Responsibilities
W. G. Sebald, The Emigrants
The Rings of Saturn
Vertigo
Aharon Shabtai, J'accuse
Hasan Shah, The Dancing Girl
C. H. Sisson, Selected Poems
Gary Snyder, Turtle Island
Muriel Spark, The Ballad of Peckham Rye
A Far Cry From Kensington
Memento Mori
George Steiner, At the New Yorker
Antonio Tabucchi, Indian Nocturne
Pereira Declares
Yoko Tawada, The Naked Eye
Dylan Thomas, A Chlld's Christmas in Wales
Collected Poems
Under Milk Wood
Uwe Timm, The Invention of Curried Sausage
Charles Tomlinson, Selected Poems
Tomas Tranströmer
The Great Enigma: New Collected Poems
Leonid Tsypkin, Summer in Baden-Baden
Tu Fu, Selected Poems
Frederic Tuten, The Adventures of Mao
Paul Valéry, Selected Writings
Enrique Vila-Matas, Bartleby & Co.
Elio Vittorini, Conversations in Sicily
Rosmarie Waldrop, Driven to Abstraction
Robert Walser, The Assistant
The Tanners
Eliot Weinberger, An Elemental Thing
Oranges and Peanuts for Sale
Nathanael West
Miss Lonelyhearts & The Day of the Locust
Tennessee Williams, Cat on a Hot Tin Roof
The Glass Menagerie
A Streetcar Named Desire
William Carlos Williams, In the American Grain
Paterson
Selected Poems
Spring and All
Louis Zukofsky, "A"
Anew

*BILINGUAL EDITION